The Encyclopedia of
Collectibles

Other Publications:

The Seafarers

World War II

The Great Cities

Home Repair and Improvement

The World's Wild Places

The Time-Life Library of Boating

Human Behavior

The Art of Sewing

The Old West

The Emergence of Man

The American Wilderness

The Time-Life Encyclopedia of Gardening

Life Library of Photography

This Fabulous Century

Foods of the World

Time-Life Library of America

Time-Life Library of Art

Great Ages of Man

Life Science Library

The Life History of the United States

Time Reading Program

Life Nature Library

Life World Library

Family Library:
   How Things Work in Your Home
   The Time-Life Book of the Family Car
   The Time-Life Family Legal Guide
   The Time-Life Book of Family Finance

The Encyclopedia of
Collectibles

Beads to Boxes

TIME-LIFE BOOKS, ALEXANDRIA, VIRGINIA

Time-Life Books Inc.
is a wholly owned subsidiary of
TIME INCORPORATED

Founder: Henry R. Luce 1898-1967

Editor-in-Chief: Hedley Donovan
Chairman of the Board: Andrew Heiskell
President: James R. Shepley
Vice Chairman: Roy E. Larsen
Corporate Editors: Ralph Graves,
Henry Anatole Grunwald

TIME-LIFE BOOKS INC.
Managing Editor: Jerry Korn
Executive Editor: David Maness
Assistant Managing Editors: Dale M. Brown,
Martin Mann, John Paul Porter (acting)
Art Director: Tom Suzuki
Chief of Research: David L. Harrison
Director of Photography: Robert G. Mason
Planning Director: Philip W. Payne (acting)
Senior Text Editor: Diana Hirsh
Assistant Art Director: Arnold C. Holeywell
Assistant Chief of Research: Carolyn L. Sackett

Chairman: Joan D. Manley
President: John D. McSweeney
Executive Vice Presidents: Carl G. Jaeger (U.S.
and Canada), David J. Walsh (International)
Vice President and Secretary: Paul R. Stewart
Treasurer and General Manager:
John Steven Maxwell
Business Manager: Peter G. Barnes
Sales Director: John L. Canova
Public Relations Director: Nicholas Benton
Personnel Director: Beatrice T. Dobie
Production Director: Herbert Sorkin
Consumer Affairs Director: Carol Flaumenhaft

The Encyclopedia of Collectibles
Editor: Betsy Frankel
Staff Writers: Michael Roberts,
Kathleen Shortall
Researchers: Judith W. Shanks,
Phyllis K. Wise
Editorial Assistant: Susan Sivard

Editorial Production
Production Editor: Douglas B. Graham
Operations Manager: Gennaro C. Esposito
Assistant Production Editor: Feliciano Madrid
Quality Control: Robert L. Young (director),
James J. Cox (assistant),
Michael G. Wight (associate)
Art Coordinator: Anne B. Landry
Copy Staff: Susan B. Galloway (chief),
Peter Kaufman, Cynthia Kleinfeld,
Ricki Tarlow, Florence Keith, Celia Beattie
Picture Department: Dolores A. Littles
Correspondents: Elisabeth Kraemer (Bonn); Margot
Hapgood, Dorothy Bacon (London); Susan Jonas,
Lucy T. Voulgaris (New York); Maria Vincenza
Aloisi, Josephine du Brusle (Paris); Ann Natanson
(Rome). Valuable assistance was also provided by
Carolyn T. Chubet, Miriam Hsia (New York).

The Encyclopedia of Collectibles
was created under the supervision
of Time-Life Books by
TREE COMMUNICATIONS, INC.
President: Rodney Friedman
Publisher: Bruce Michel
Vice President: Ronald Gross
Secretary: Paul Levin

The Encyclopedia of Collectibles
Managing Editor: Andrea DiNoto
Text Director: Jay Gold
Art Director: Sara Burris, Marsha Gold
Photographers: David Arky, Steven Mays
Assistant Editors: Cathy Cashion, Linda Campbell
Franklin, Barbara Moynehan
Researchers: Anna-Teresa Callen,
Mary Clarke, Patricia Ellis, Dennis Southers
Designers: Christopher Jones, Barbara Weiss
Administrative Assistant: Eva Gold
Writers: Hyla Clark, Mary Mac Franklin, Fridolf
Johnson, William C. Ketchum Jr., Robert K. Liu,
Joan McCullough, Rebecca Mayer, Jerry E.
Patterson, Burton Spiller, J. Garrison Stradling,
Joan and James Theobald

Consultants for this volume: Harmer Johnson,
Manuel Keene, Valrae Reynolds, James Romano
(Beads); Ernie Oest (Beer Cans); Phillip H. Curtis,
James R. Mitchell (Belleek); Gene Kosche, J.
Garrison Stradling (Bennington); Arnold Ehlert
(Bibles); Don Berkebile (Bicycles); Robert Nikirk
(Books); John Brindle (Botanical Prints); Jim
Whetzel (Bottles); Don Maust (Boxes)

The Cover: A mouth-watering array of beer cans,
both domestic and foreign, includes examples
prized for either rarity or beauty.

Acknowledgments: The editors wish to thank: Don
Adams, Ed Gerling, Dr. Richard Walter Jeanes,
Vince Pigott, Irene Rouse, Henry A. Siegel, L.
Elsinore Springer, Virginia Theological Seminary.
Page 21, courtesy J. F. Concoff; pages 36-37,
courtesy P. Ellmann; page 48, and Horsefeathers
bell, page 53, courtesy G. H. Nader; Bennington
spittoon, page 60, courtesy The Stradlings; Bruce
Rogers Bible, page 78, courtesy Seven Gables
Bookshop; Book of John, page 78, courtesy Rare
Book Division, The New York Public Library,
Astor, Lenox and Tilden Foundations; pages 92-
93, courtesy P. Magarick; pages 96-97, courtesy F.
Johnson; pages 98, 99, 101, and *Lewis and Clarke
Journal*, page 102, collection of C. J. Tanenbaum;
other books, pages 102-103, courtesy Swann
Galleries, Inc.; pages 104-106, courtesy Crossroads
of Sport; page 107, courtesy Rare Book Division,
The New York Public Library, Astor, Lenox and
Tilden Foundations; pages 108-111, courtesy
Seven Gables Bookshop; pages 112-117, courtesy
P. Magarick; wood candlebox, page 148, courtesy
Mrs. J. E. Brown; brass candlebox, page 148,
courtesy Mr. and Mrs. C. V. Hagler; knife box,
page 148, coffer, page 149, lacquer teabox, page
150, courtesy W. Hodges; salt and sugar boxes and
open caddy, page 150, courtesy Mrs. J. E. Brown;
octagonal caddy, page 150, courtesy American
Institute of Architects; Conestoga toolbox, page
152, courtesy Mrs. J. E. Brown; bride's box, page
152, courtesy Mrs. E. M. Galban; Bible box, page
153, courtesy W. Hodges; closed lap desk, page
153, courtesy Mrs. M. F. Minich; tortoise-shell
snuffbox, page 155, courtesy Mrs. J. E. Brown;
Dutch tobacco box and tole snuffbox, page 155,
courtesy W. Hodges; piqué snuffbox, page
155, courtesy Mrs. E. M. Galban; vinaigrette, page
159, courtesy Mrs. J. E. Brown; pillbox, page 159,
courtesy Mrs. J. G. Carswell; Tyrolean box, page
160, courtesy Mrs. H. B. Madry.

Contents

6 **Beads**

22 **Beer Cans**

34 **Belleek Porcelain**

46 **Bells**

56 **Bennington Pottery**

68 **Bibles**

80 **Bicycles**

92 **Books**

118 **Botanical Prints**

130 **Bottles**

146 **Boxes**

Beads
Ornaments from Everywhere

Why should beads, which are nothing but baubles of varying sizes and shapes with holes in them, provoke such enthusiasm among collectors? The answer, in large part, is expressed in one word: history. Beads have been made and worn for at least the past 30,000 years in all cultures and in all parts of the world. Stone Age women wore bead collars made from stone or bone, and Siberians of 10,000 years ago wore bead necklaces of ivory from the tusks of the now-extinct hairy mammoth. The ancient Egyptians used collars of beads, and the Indians of the New World made beads a form of art. Beads have

Robert Liu is the founder and editor of the quarterly publication, "The Bead Journal." A medical researcher and writer by profession, he became seriously involved in bead collecting seven years ago.

been used for millennia as religious talismans and aids to prayer and as coinage. A single old bead, in short, can resound with echoes from man's history. Beads also fascinate by their almost infinite variety, their beauty and the ingenuity that has gone into making them.

The long history behind beads, as well as the world-wide commerce in them as items of trade and a medium of exchange, introduces some unusual complications for collectors. Modern copies continue to be made of many old and interesting sorts of beads and these recent beads are difficult to tell from the genuinely old. To cite one by no means unusual case: around the beginning of this century manufacturers in India supplied a fertility bead amulet called a *talhatana* to Arab traders who sold them to the Tuareg nomads of the northern Sahara. These amulets were handmade from the reddish variety of quartz called carnelian. Thereupon, the Tuareg copied the design for themselves, using silver instead of carnelian. Later, German manufacturers started making the amulet beads of carnelian, but shaped by power tools.

These richly colorful strands of glass beads include several varieties of "African" beads, some of which were made in Europe and used to trade with Africans. The large green beads in the middle are Venetian millefiori—containing bouquet-like clusters of flowers. Two rows below the millefiori are red glass beads imitating carnelian.

The Czechs went into mass production of the same beads with molded glass, and soon other European manufacturers made cheap plastic copies. The most plentiful *talhatana* today are the plastic imitations. A collector, needless to say, prefers the amulets handcrafted in India, or silver ones made by the Tuareg, to the plastic copies, which are mere curiosities of little value.

As if such commercial twists are not puzzling enough, trading practices that began long ago and still continue tangle the identification of beads further yet. Beads sold in an area tend to be linked to that area, regardless of their origin. African beads, for example, are popular among many collectors. However, most were not made in Africa—although African craftsmen have long made beads from nuts and shells and, more recently, from glass obtained through a unique recycling process; the local bead makers grind up European beads, empty beer bottles and medicine jars, put the powder into molds and fire the molds in clay ovens. Most beads collected as African are quite different—beads made in Europe that white traders took to Africa as barter for gold, ivory and palm-nut oil. They include the millefiori beads made in the glassmaking center of Murano, an island in Venice's lagoon, and others made in the late 19th and early 20th centuries in the glass factories of the Netherlands, Czechoslovakia and Italy. Many of these African beads have recently been gathered in Africa and shipped back to Europe—and to America—to satisfy the current enthusiasm for "ethnic" jewelry; since they are readily available, they are good buys for budding collectors.

The bead trade reached not just Africa, but also across the Atlantic to the New World. Long before Columbus, the Indians made their own beads of shell, bone, stone, clay and metal. Later, the Spanish conquistadors traded beads with the Incas; the English and French with the Indians of North America. Among collectors, North American beads are grouped according to geographic area or tribe: opaque-white glass beads from Italy are linked with the San Joaquin Valley of California; "Hubbell" beads, named for the trader who sold these Czech imitations of turquoise, with Arizona and the Southwest; polychrome Venetian beads, with the Plains Indians, especially the Crow of Montana;

All of the beads above date from 1500 B.C. to 600 A.D. and are made of the ceramic called faïence. The four strands at left come from Persia. The other strands were made in Egypt; the deep-blue bead is intended to resemble lapis lazuli, the others turquoise.

The ancient Middle Eastern beads above are made of semiprecious stones: amazonite and lapis lazuli (top row); agate, carnelian and quartz (middle row); and onyx (bottom).

This glass, juglike bead, pitted by age, was made in Syria, probably around 100 A.D.

old Dutch beads, with East Coast Indian sites; "seed" beads from Italy and Czechoslovakia, with the various Indians who used them to decorate their clothing.

To unravel these snarls and get an idea of the age and value of a bead you may be looking at, you need to know some of the history of bead manufacture. The earliest beads, of course, were made of natural substances with holes drilled in them—bone, teeth, stones or sea shells. Such beads are produced even today by tribal people as yet little touched by Western technology.

Among the first people to use man-made substances for beads were the Egyptians, who came up first with faïence in 4500 B.C. and then with glass. Egyptian faïence is a ceramic not to be confused with tin-glazed earthenware of the same name originally made in Faenza, Italy. Egyptian faïence was made by heating quartz crystals with lime and sodium carbonate, plus copper to color the beads blue, or manganese for purple. The mixture, fired in molds, produced lovely beads that resembled two semiprecious stones, lapis lazuli and turquoise, and thus were much in demand in the Mediterranean basin and were widely copied there.

After the faïence process had been in use some 3,000 years, by around 1500 B.C., the Egyptians perfected the manufacture of glass, which is more malleable than faïence. Sand was fired with potassium carbonate or potassium nitrate. While still soft, the glass was made into rods and wound around metal wires or tubes. The result: glass beads with a hole for stringing them. The Egyptians soon went on to produce "eye" beads with a spot of contrasting color in them. Other Middle Eastern artisans made a further improvement, fabricating what are today called millefiori, Italian for "thousand flowers." A bundle of thin glass rods of various colors was fused into a single "cane," then sliced like a salami. The slices were then embedded in a semimolten piece of glass and fused there, the bead looking like a bouquet of tiny, many-hued flowers. The Syrians and Egyptians 1,000 years later took this technique its last step, arranging glass rods so that when fused by heat the image of a face appeared with hair, eyes and even teeth. The rods were again sliced into sections and fused into a piece of molten glass. A collector who discovers a Roman face bead has found a great rarity.

Bead making also flourished in Asia. Among the finest beads from the Far East are Chinese enamel and cloisonné, some made with gilded wire. Japanese craftsmen also made interesting beads of glass and cloisonné. Perhaps the most precious of Asian beads are the etched agate *tzi* beads and turquoise from Tibet, both of which were believed to have magical properties.

You can find all these beads, from all parts of the world, sold widely in the United States. A brief glance at "beads" in the Yellow Pages of the telephone directory will tell which firms are selling "novelties" for the dress trade and which deal in the beads collectors want. An-

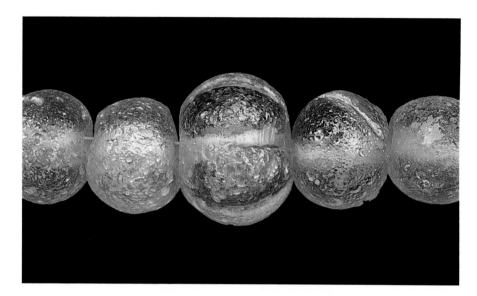

Ancient glass beads from Turkey (left) display an iridescence that results from the decomposition of the surface, damage probably caused by exposure to damp soil or humidity.

Roman face beads, shown here larger than actual size, reveal astonishing detail. The eyes, mouth and other features were made by fusing rods of differently colored glass with heat, then slicing the fused rods and embedding the slices in glass beads. Invented by Syrians and Egyptians during Roman times, the technique spread through the ancient world; these are probably from Syria. They show the pitting of age, although the corroded areas have been partly restored by grinding to a smooth finish.

tique shows and big flea markets usually include bead dealers and traders who specialize in antique or ethnic jewelry. Importers of African and Asian crafts frequently carry beads. And once you are recognized as a collector among bead fanciers and dealers, other avenues open up. As my enthusiasm became known, a variety of part-time dealers began to call on me at home—ex-Peace Corps members who had picked up beads in the Middle East, peripatetic students back from Asia, foot-loose professors with European beads to sell.

While a varied collection of interesting beads is not difficult to assemble, it will have little value unless you organize it; a miscellaneous jumble brings little enjoyment to its owner and is almost worthless on sale. Label all acquisitions, tying on a tag that shows where and when you obtained the beads, what you paid, where the bead appears to have been made, and when. This should be done promptly after purchase; after only a

short lapse of time it is easy to mix together beads of similar appearance but different origin.

Although bead collecting need not be an expensive pursuit, it can escalate. One of my few ventures into the higher realms of collecting was as exciting as a horse race—and fortunately paid off like a winning ticket on a long shot. A remarkable collection of a wealthy Minnesotan—the largest offering of ancient beads in recent times, especially rich in Roman face beads and millefiori—was on the auction block. A friend and I bid on two of the 80 or so lots of necklaces. We were successful on just one bid and it was fortunate that we did not win more, for it was difficult to raise the $625 for this necklace of 11 face beads. That was in 1972. A few years later face beads in decent condition sold for $200 each.

For related material, see the articles on Handbags, Jade and Jewelry in separate volumes of this encyclopedia.

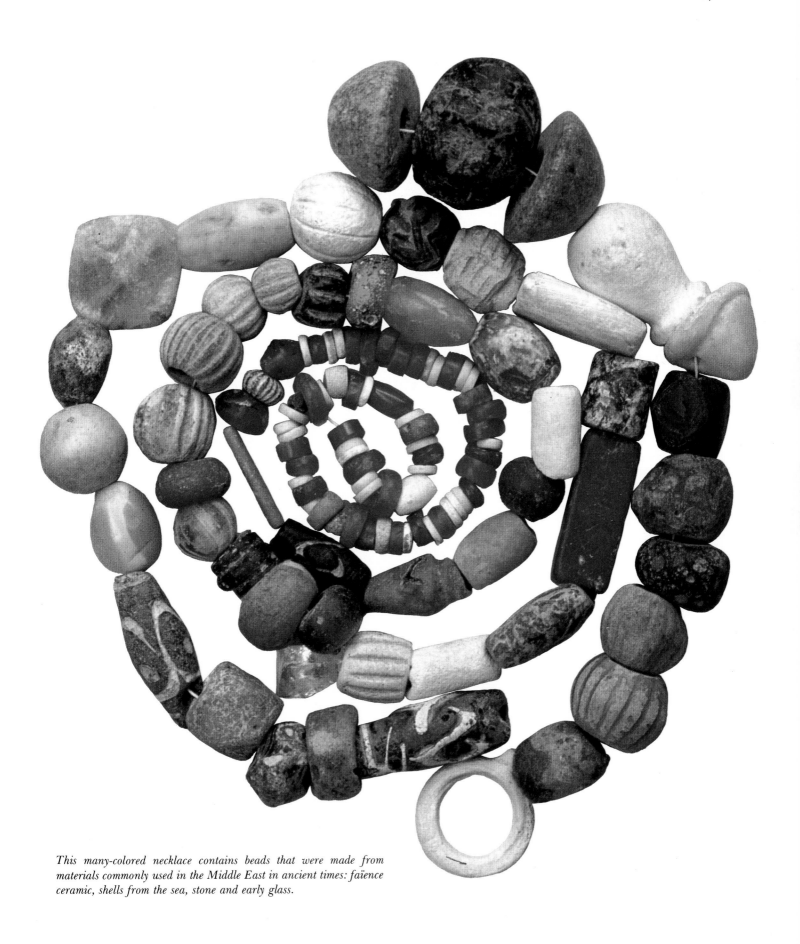

This many-colored necklace contains beads that were made from materials commonly used in the Middle East in ancient times: faïence ceramic, shells from the sea, stone and early glass.

Although most African beads are from Europe, some, like these, were made locally. The two beige strands above at left are land-snail shell; the black beads, palm-nut shell; the white, ostrich-egg shell.

African shells used for beads include the large Arca—the rectangles —and the whorled Conus (bottom). The Conus at left and the Arca at the top are real shells worked in Africa; the others are copies.

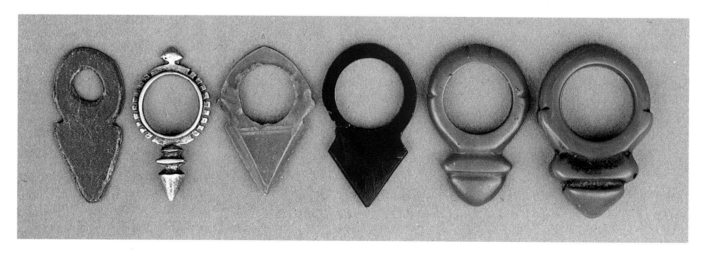

Six talhatana, fertility amulets worn by the Tuareg nomads of the Sahara, differ in size and in origin. From the left they are: a crude imitation made of plastic, a silver specimen made by Tuareg silver-smiths, a carnelian version from India, a carnelian copy made in Bavaria and two differing plastic copies. Though they are shaped like rings, the amulets are normally worn as pendants.

This African necklace, found in the United Republic of Cameroon, consists of beads made in Europe. The orange-colored beads are probably of Czech origin. The others are of a type produced in the late 19th or early 20th Century in Venice. They are called chevron beads because of the V-shaped decoration, formed by grinding through multicolored layers of glass.

Companions for Beads

Work lavished on ojimes, Japanese fasteners, is visible in the four above. The ivory example (left) is carved to look like frolicking puppies. The tall ojime is decorated with gold sea grass and a crab. The pink coral one depicts a sage, Daruma. The round ojime has a floral pattern in silver. Ojimes have brought up to $4,000 each at auction.

Bead fanciers collect a variety of small objects that are not beads but resemble them in size and beauty of workmanship. Among the favorites are the Japanese *ojime (left)*, which are meticulously crafted fasteners made for the small carrying cases, called *inro*, that the Japanese used to suspend from their waists.

Bead collectors also favor spindle whorls *(below, left)*, which have been used in many cultures as an aid in twisting yarn. Many spindle whorls are made of terra cotta, although stone, metal, bone, faïence and glass have also been used. Spindle whorls that are made in the Americas often are beautifully incised with animal or geometric motifs.

Other small collectibles include tiny Egyptian amulets that represent various ancient Egyptian gods *(below)* or scarabs, which are stylized images of the Egyptians' sacred beetle. Many Egyptian artifacts of this type were made of faïence, as are modern imitations.

These New World spindle whorls antedate Columbus' arrival. The small ones were used for delicate fibers such as cotton; the larger for coarse fibers such as agave. The whorl with the face is from Ecuador, the others from Mexico and Colombia.

The faïence figure (right) is a djed, a symbol of the Egyptian god Osiris. At left is Toth, the ibis-headed god of learning.

Strings of Chinese beads of the type known as Peking or Canton glass display their identifying characteristics: bright and varied color, traces of clay and air bubbles inside, and irregular contours.

These beads look like turquoise and copal (right), coral (middle row) and polished, incised stone (left), but they are clever fakes made of glass and plastic in the late 19th or early 20th Century.

Chinese enamel beads and those with gold inlaid on the enamel, called cloisonné (above, right), are among the most delicate of all beads. They were made in the last century, when geometric designs were popular, along with floral designs and Chinese dragons (bottom, left).

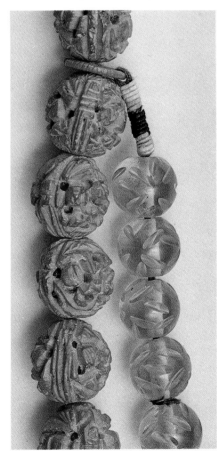

The brown beads on this modern Chinese necklace are carved fruit pits. Cut-glass beads form a side dangle.

Seed beads decorate the front and form the fringe at the bottom of the leather Arapaho bag above, made about 1900. The beadwork shines partly because some of the tiny beads were faceted metal.

This curious combination of a bag and a garment is slipped over the head, with the fringed carrying pouch worn over the hip. It was made of woven beadwork by Ojibway Indians about 1885.

Beadwork covers the upper portions of handsome moccasins made by a Sioux artisan about 1900. Such elaborately decorated items were undoubtedly reserved for ceremonial occasions.

Masterpieces of American Indian Beadwork

The American Indians were masters of beadwork—decorating clothing and other articles with beads—long before the Europeans landed in Massachusetts and Virginia. For this purpose Indians originally used native materials such as shells, stones and even dyed hollow porcupine quills. But when the Europeans brought seed beads—so called because of their tiny size—for trading purposes, the Indian craftworkers attained new heights of artistry, producing with skill and imagination a remarkable flowering in the decorative arts that continued until recently.

Working with seed beads spread to Indians in most parts of the country, but the masters remained the Indians native to the Eastern woodlands, the Great Lakes area and the Plains. Women did the beadwork, using two techniques: sewing beads to cloth or leather backings, or weaving beads so that the entire fabric was made simply of beads and the weaving threads.

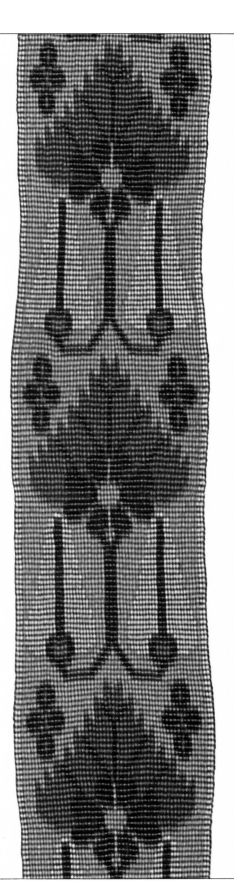

The Crow beadwork shirt above, made about 1890, slips over the head like a poncho, with the horsehair tassels in front.

A beaded band (right) copies garter-like legging ties that were worn by the Menominee on festive occasions.

The left and center strands shown above are from the Philippines and Thailand; their ages are unknown. The right strand is from Indone-sia, where the Dayak people revere such deep-red beads; they date from the 11th Century.

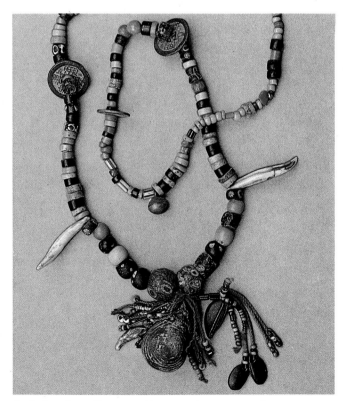

An Indonesian talisman necklace contains, among other components, old Chinese coins and a bell, three teeth and European trade beads.

A Bedouin necklace from North Africa includes Turkish coins, two hand amulets and beads of amber and glass.

European-made "cane beads" found in Peru are named for their shape. They are from the 16th or 17th Century and are blue on top, *white underneath and black inside. The Peruvian Indians acquired such glass beads in trade with their Spanish conquerors.*

A pendant of clear quartz dating from before Columbus' voyage of 1492 is the central element in a modern silver necklace. The green *stones are granite-like Central American metadiorite. The designer did not alter the quartz; antique pendants lose their value if changed.*

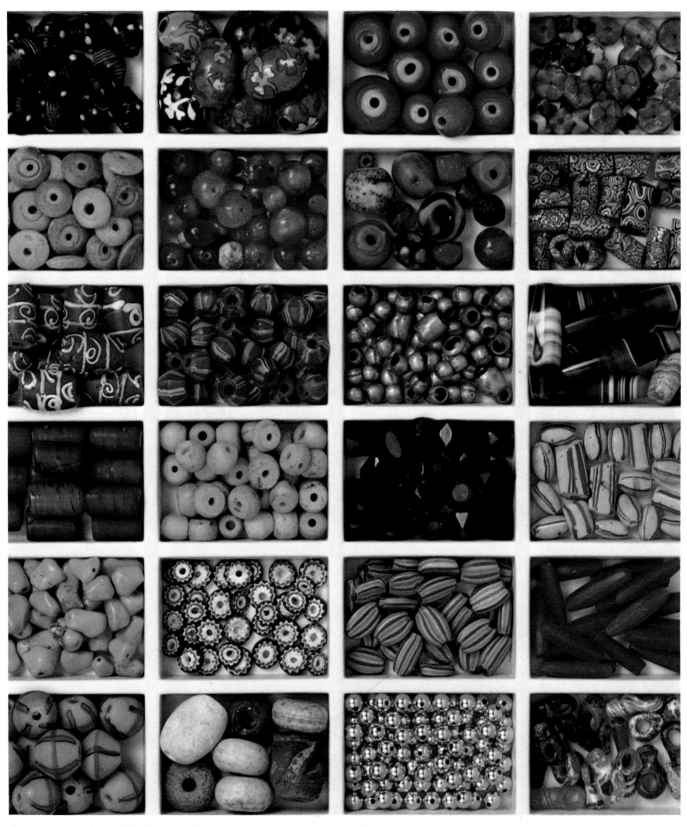

A compartmented tray like this is indispensable for sorting beads. Most of these ancient and contemporary beads were recent imports from Africa to be used in jewelry. Colored glass beads, most of which originated in Italy, surround Chinese cloisonné enamel (second column, top), simulated carnelian called Cornaline d'Aleppo (third column, top) and silver Ethiopian beads (third column, third row).

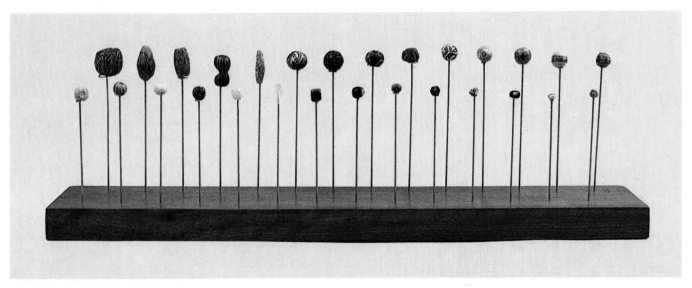

Brass rods mounted on a walnut board provide a dramatic setting to display individual beads close up. Various groupings within the exhibition can be emphasized by changing the height and spacing of the rods, or by making a choice specimen stand above the others.

MUSEUMS
American Museum of Natural History
New York, N.Y. 10024

Corning Museum of Glass
Corning, N.Y. 14830

Denver Museum of Natural History
Denver, Colorado 80205

Field Museum of Natural History
Chicago, Illinois 60605

Maxwell Museum of Anthropology
University of New Mexico
Albuquerque, New Mexico 87131

Metropolitan Museum of Art
New York, N.Y. 10028

Museum of Fine Arts
Boston, Massachusetts 02115

Museum of the American Indian
New York, N.Y. 10032

Natural History Museum of Los Angeles County
Los Angeles, California 90007

Portland Art Museum
Portland, Oregon 97205

The University Museum
University of Pennsylvania
Philadelphia, Pennsylvania 19174

COLLECTORS ORGANIZATIONS
The Bead Society

P.O. Box 605
Venice, California 90219

Northern California Bead Society
1580 B Solano Avenue
Albany, California 94707

PERIODICALS
The Bead Journal, P.O. Box 24C47, Los Angeles,
California 90024

BOOKS
Beck, Horace C., *Classification and Nomenclature of Beads and Pendants,* Liberty Cap Books, 1928.
(Reprinted 1973)

Erikson, Joan M., *The Universal Bead,* Norton,
1969.

Orchard, William C., *Beads and Beadwork of the American Indian,* Museum of the American Indian,
1975.

Seyd, Mary, *Introducing Beads,* Watson-Guptill
Publications, 1973.

van der Sleen, W. G. N., *A Handbook on Beads,*
Liberty Cap Books, 1973.

Archaeological Research Booklets, Vols. I-X, G. B.
Fenstermaker, 1974-1977.

Kidd, Kenneth E. and Martha A., *A Classification System for Glass Beads for the Use of Field Archaeologists. Canadian Historic Sites: Occasional Papers in Archaeology and History,* No. 1. Publishing
Centre, Ottawa, 1970.

Beer Cans
Valued Empties

I got hooked on beer cans during my senior year at Yale. I found myself competing with beer-drinking classmates to see who would be first to fill the ledges beneath the ceilings of our dormitory rooms with empties. My group won the contest—and I kept on collecting. By commencement I had accumulated 280 cans from all over the country. A little more than a decade later, I owned 11,000 different cans, including what I realized by then were among the world's rarest specimens. And my calling card identified me as the "world's largest beer can collector."

It was a rather solitary hobby until October 1969, when a St. Louis newspaper ran a feature story on a

---

John Ahrens' collection of more than 11,000 beer cans earned him mention in the Guinness Book of World Records. Ahrens is a publishing executive and lives in Mount Laurel, New Jersey.

---

collector named Denver M. Wright Jr. Five men who read the article discovered to their delight that they were not alone in their passion for beer cans. They got in touch with Wright, and the next year the group formed the Beer Can Collectors of America *(page 26)*. Organization made the avocation respectable, bringing in others (including myself) who had been pursuing the hobby in isolation for years.

Within a decade, the association had enrolled 13,000 members all over the world, each ranked according to the size of his collection. Anyone who has acquired from 500 to 749 different cans, for instance, is classified as a journeyman brewer and is awarded three stars on the roster. At the top of the scale are five-star grand brewmasters, each of whom owns more than 1,000 cans.

Through the organization, collectors are able to share information on preserving cans and restoring damaged ones. The association also fosters standards of fair conduct in trading, and does everything in its power—often to no avail—to keep members from dealing in cans for

Brewing nations all over the globe are represented in a display of the author's favorite foreign specimens. Many American collectors consider cans produced abroad to be more beautiful and intriguing than those manufactured in the United States.

money. Its "News Report" furnishes information on the state of the beer industry, with tables listing each major brewer's output. The report also keeps up with such oddities as a drowning that occurred when a man jumped off a yacht to retrieve a can, and a murder in which the weapon was a six-pack.

Can collecting is a new pursuit because the cans are a relatively recent innovation. Solid foods were canned in the 19th Century, soup and soft drinks before World War I. But aside from a few unmarketed experiments, there was no beer in cans until January 24, 1935, when Krueger's Finest Beer *(page 28)* and Krueger's Cream Ale went to market in 12-ounce, plastic-lined steel cans along with the first triangular-bladed opener, now a popular collectible, too. Within six months, Krueger's sales multiplied more than five times, and larger breweries began to edge warily into the market. (Pabst offered its canned brew in a container labeled Export but filled with the identical beer the company was selling in bottles as Blue Ribbon.)

These first successful cans are desirable—some have reportedly been sold for several hundred dollars—and every change in can manufacture since has introduced a prize collectible. Some breweries made a transition to cans by offering cone-top cans, which could be filled and capped like bottles on existing assembly lines. But cone-tops were unpopular because, unlike flat-tops, they could not be stacked in the refrigerator. By the 1960s they were virtually extinct. More than a decade later, an unscrupulous dealer tried to capitalize on their rarity by peddling bogus cone-tops. Sophisticated collectors easily spotted them as fakes, though, because the brewer's address printed on the cans included a zip code, which was not in general use until the late 1960s.

When aluminum cans were developed in the late 1950s, one brewery, Primo Beer of Hawaii, issued them with paper labels. But this experiment was soon abandoned. Pull tabs, introduced in 1962, were in use on 70 per cent of all cans within three years. In 1965, the tab was replaced with a ring for easier gripping.

Among other developments that affect collecting were legal changes. Until March 1, 1950, a federal regulation required the words "Internal Revenue Tax Paid" to be stamped on each can. The presence of that phrase, which collectors abbreviate to IRTP, is one way to determine that the can was made before 1950.

A few cans are also dated by slogans touting the health-giving properties of the beverages they contained. Such claims were prohibited, state by state, between 1935 and 1945. Among the resultant collector's items are a Schlitz can boasting of "Sunshine Vitamin D" and a Storz-ette can proclaiming the benefits of its "beerette" to weight-conscious women.

While most technological advances were perfected in the United States, British brewers took the lead in offering consumers a choice of sizes, particularly extra-large party cans. The first appeared in the mid-1950s (American versions came along about a decade later) in two sizes: 7 pints and 4 pints. And from 1966 to 1972, Tollemache & Cobbold toyed with archaic measures, offering a can containing half a firkin.

As progress and experimentation were making some cans scarce, so were the vicissitudes of the beer business. Of the 800 or so breweries operating in the United States when beer was first being marketed in cans, more than 650 had gone out of business by 1975. Drinkers long since may have forgotten such local or regional brands as Spearman Straight Eight (Pensacola, Florida) and Fesenmeier's (Huntington, West Virginia), but the cans that they were sold in become increasingly valuable to collectors as the years go by.

Rarity can also be created by historical events. The camouflaged cans of World War II *(page 28)*, scattered by the millions over Asia and Europe, are now avidly sought. So is the can issued in 1969 by the Felinfoel Brewery of Llanelly, Wales, to mark the investiture of Britain's Prince Charles as Prince of Wales, a fact that was printed in English and Welsh on the label. Only 24 of the cans are known to have reached the United States.

Instant relics are also created when beer-can labels run into legal troubles. In 1976, Amana Beer was introduced by a Minnesota brewery for sale in the region of Iowa populated by the Amana religious society. Within a week, the society won an injunction against the use of its name. Can dealers rushed to buy unsold stocks for resale: almost every collector wanted an Amana can.

If you do not seek rarities, can collecting is inexpensive, especially if you confine your acquisitions to one of several broad categories. Some collectors concentrate on either full cans, empties or flats (unfinished cans in the form of unrolled, printed sheets). Others accumulate only cans of a certain age or nationality, cans produced in sets or unusual sizes, or cans whose contents they have consumed. And, while many are purists dedicated to cans and nothing else, some are equally eager to find other "breweriana" such as trays, mugs, bottles, calendars, coasters, labels and signs.

Where should you look first? My advice is to head for the nearest dump. Combing trash heaps is the fastest and least expensive way to find old cans, and a good supply of "dumpers" will give you cans to trade with other collectors. After dumps, the next places to look are roadside ditches, garbage cans and storerooms of abandoned taverns. In 1973, I visited a local warehouse that had been a brewery years earlier. While showing me around, the manager went off for a while. He came back with a beautiful quart-sized Esslinger cone-top, which he handed to me. The warehouse owners had discovered it

Three stages in the evolution of the beer can: On the left, a seamed, three-piece can from the 1930s that carries detailed directions for opening it; at center, one of the now-extinct cone-tops, made from the '30s through the early '50s; at right, a modern pull-tab can.

when they moved in and were using it and several others to store turpentine. A collector I know looks inside the walls of vacated buildings because he has found that carpenters who are working on walls often nail up empties inside rather than carrying them to a trash bin. He also had success looking in the rafters of abandoned firehouses and railroad stations. Other collectors search around picnic sites, caves and other places frequented by hunters or campers.

Shop for local brands wherever you travel. You will not find much variety in wine-drinking countries such as Spain or Italy, but there will be many to choose among in Britain, Germany, Sweden and Denmark. If you have accommodating friends and relatives, ask them to collect for you when they travel overseas. Send along an opener and clear, precise instructions for opening, draining and packing the cans and mailing them home to you. Each can should be wrapped separately in newspaper and packed tightly in a strong box, such as a whiskey case.

And of course, you must keep a sharp lookout, wherever you are, for the sort of error that makes an ordinary item special. I once went into a delicatessen and spotted on its shelves a six-pack of malt liquor containing a can on which only half a label had been printed.

Long-distance shipping and expeditions to the dump are sure to leave you with some cans that need restoration. Small dents can sometimes be popped out by hand or with a small instrument. Larger dents can often be removed by filling the can with water and putting it into the freezer. The water expands as it turns to ice, pushing the dents out. An extremely rusted can might as well be thrown away, but if good metal remains, rub the rusted parts with emery paper. Oxalic acid, available at pharmacies, may work better if the condition is particularly bad. Some collectors retouch damaged parts of the printed surface with metallic or enamel paints.

GUIDELINES FOR CAN COLLECTORS

Tips to help in trading beer cans with fellow collectors are contained in these tables, which are based on information compiled by the Beer Can Collectors of America, whose insignia is reproduced below. The first table offers guidelines for establishing the relative values of cans of various sizes, ages and countries of issue, using as a measure a can currently being made and sold in the United States. According to this table, for instance, one current foreign can is worth two current U.S. cans, but if the foreign can is obsolete its value is four current U.S. cans. A second table lists procedures for trading cans by mail. A third table lists abbreviations used to advertise cans, while a fourth summarizes criteria collectors use to grade the condition of cans on a scale of 1 to 5.

WHAT CANS ARE WORTH IN TRADE

CAN TO BE TRADED	VALUE (current U.S. cans)
Current U.S. can, all sizes through 16 oz.	1
Obsolete U.S. can from the 1960s or 1970s	2
Current foreign can	2
Obsolete U.S. can from the 1950s	4
Obsolete foreign can	4
Obsolete U.S. can from the 1940s (label must state "Internal Revenue Tax Paid")	6
U.S. cone-top can (cone-tops from the 1930s may be worth more)	8
Obsolete U.S. can from the 30s	8
Current U.S. gallon can	8
World War II olive-drab can	10
Foreign gallon can	16
Obsolete quart cone- or spout-top can	16
Obsolete U.S. gallon can	20

CHECKLIST FOR TRADING BY MAIL

List cans in alphabetical order, usually by brand name rather than by brewery.

List foreign cans separately from U.S. cans.

When possible, give the year of the can's issue.

Note the condition of the can, using the official grading table *(right);* otherwise cans are assumed to be in good condition.

Note the size of the can; otherwise the can is assumed to be the standard 12-ounce size.

When possible, open cans from the bottom.

Pack cans carefully to prevent damage in transit.

BEER-CAN ABBREVIATIONS

TYPES OF BEER:

A Ale	GB Ginger Beer	ML Malt Liquor
B Beer	HH Half & Half	P Porter
BB Bock Beer	LC Low-Calorie	PB Pilsener Beer
DA Draft Ale	Beer	ST Stout
DB Draft Beer	NB Near Beer	MLA Malt Lager

TYPES OF CAN:

AA All Aluminum	SL Seamless	SS Soldered Seam
AT Aluminum Top	TT Tab-Top	WS Welded Seam
CT Cone-Top	FL Flat-Top	ES Epoxy-cemented Seam

DESCRIPTION:

GC Good Condition	D Dented
FC Fair Condition	R Rusty
PC Poor Condition	VR Very Rusty
CP Current Production	W/OT Without Top
OP Obsolete Production	W/OB Without Bottom
OB Out of Business	Res Restored

HOW COLLECTORS GRADE CAN CONDITION

GRADE 1 = EXCELLENT
Can looks new. It contains top and bottom, but may have triangular holes made by the standard "church key" opener. No rust, scratches, fading, dents or imperfections are visible on any side.

GRADE 2 = GOOD
Can may have shallow surface scratches, small nicks and slight dimples, but no rust.

GRADE 3 = AVERAGE
Can may have light rust, scratches, nicks, dimples or fading. Front is in good condition but back may be poor.

GRADE 4 = FAIR
Can has all the defects of Grade 3 but in more severe form, and is barely good enough for display, and should be replaced when a better specimen comes along. Sometimes a Grade 4 can is restorable to Grade 3.

GRADE 5 = POOR
Can is rusted or faded and label is indistinguishable or almost so. Not suitable for display or trading, and not restorable.

Cans like these three—containing less than the usual 12 ounces—have become increasingly popular with beer drinkers, but they are still unusual and collectors seek them.

The Koch's gallon can, shown with a standard 12-ouncer, was sold from about 1965 to 1973. It was no match for the six-pack, which beer drinkers found more convenient and less wasteful.

The Art of Opening

Collectors may not care about where the beer inside a valuable can winds up, but they are quite particular about the manner in which it is removed.

With the old-fashioned seamed cans, which collectors still find intact fairly often in tavern storerooms, the standard triangular opener called a church key can be used. Openings should always be made on the bottom, so that the punctures will be concealed when the can is displayed.

Modern seamless cans, which have no bottom rim to provide leverage for the standard opener, are more easily punctured with the professional press-type opener shown below. This instrument was originally made for bartenders and was a standard barroom fixture before the advent of tab-opening cans. An ice pick will also serve the purpose adequately, but its use requires considerable care to avoid injury to can and collector.

Its barroom heyday over, the press-type opener is still used by collectors.

Krueger's "K-man" appeared on the world's first beer can in 1935. Krueger used the design until 1942—this can is from 1940.

Pabst Export cans are rare because the brand name was used just long enough to test public reaction to canned beer.

Produced for only two years, the Schlitz Lager cone-top was the first of its kind. It was designed to resemble the company's bottle.

The Coronation Brew can, issued in England to mark the start of King George VI's reign in 1937, is among the world's rarest.

Camouflaged cans from World War II are scarce because GIs discarded them on distant fighting fronts in Europe and Asia.

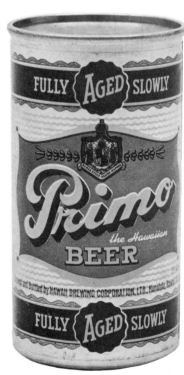

Launched in Hawaii in 1958, canned Primo beer left the market within a year. The can had a paper label and concave top.

Only one collection is known to include this design, one of many issued by a food-store chain from the mid-1950s to the late 1970s.

Old Georgetown's can pinpointed some of the sights of Washington, D.C., including the site of the Christian Heurich brewery.

Soul cans have fetched up to $225 because of a rumor (false) that the brewery was destroyed in race riots in Los Angeles.

A Pittsburgh disc jockey's whimsical invention of Olde Frothingslosh inspired a local brewer to produce a real beer by that name.

Playmate, marketed in the early 1960s, was withdrawn when Playboy Enterprises sued, claiming exclusive right to the trademark.

Though it was introduced at the height of the James Bond movie craze, 007 flopped grandly, offering collectors another rarity.

The cans on these two pages are treasured not for their rarity, but because they are outstanding examples of labeling art. Directly at right are the chaste blue-and-gold label of the now-defunct Cremo Brewing Company of New Britain, Connecticut, and a colorful historical scene issued by the Lafayette Brewery of Lafayette, Indiana.

Below, two cans that received the annual design award given by the Beer Can Collectors of America in 1975 and 1977 flank a 1950s Fox Head label that surely would have been a winner if the prize had been in existence then. On the opposite page are Japanese cans from Asahi and Suntory that use photographs of nature and are among the world's prettiest beer-can designs.

In 1976 many breweries across the United States put out special editions, like the five at left, to commemorate the Bicentennial year.

The can at far right, from Ortlieb of Philadelphia, commemorates a local institution—the annual Mummers' Day parade.

This flat sheet of printed metal, ready to be formed into cans, is part of a wildlife series that Schmidt has been adding to for about 20 years. Such "flats" are becoming scarce as canmakers turn to a process that prints labels on formed round cans.

Like all beer cans issued in sets, the Kentucky Derby winners series was quickly sought by collectors when it was introduced. The series, honoring 15 Derby champions, was produced in 1977 by the Sterling Brothers brewery (now owned by Heileman) of Evansville, Indiana.

Drewry's of South Bend, Indiana, gave collectors 12 prize labels when it issued a series displaying the signs of the zodiac in 1955.

COLLECTORS ORGANIZATIONS
Beer Can Collectors of America
747 Merus Court
Fenton, Missouri 63026

World Wide Beer Can Collectors
P.O. Box 1852
Independence, Missouri 64055

BOOKS
Beer Can Collectors of America, The:
The Beer Can: A Complete Guide to Beer Can Collecting. Greatlakes Living Press, 1976.

Guide to United States Beer Cans. Greatlakes Living Press, 1975.

Bussell, Darrold, *Foreign Beer Cans.* Wallace-Homestead Book Company, 1977.

Cady, Lew, *Beer Can Collecting.* Tempo Books, 1976.

Dolphin, Richard R., *Collecting Beer Cans: A World Guide.* Bounty Books, 1977.

Martells, Jack:
The Beer Can Collector's Bible. Ballantine Books, 1976.
The Cone Top Collector's Bible. Greatlakes Living Press, 1976.

A duck taking off from a marsh adorns a dish 8 inches square, made about 1888 by Ott and Brewer, first American potters to produce Belleek.

Belleek Porcelain
Turn-of-the-Century Fancies

Along with fine linen, sparkling crystal and a heady malt beverage called stout, Ireland has given the world an exquisite eggshell-thin china called Belleek. Known for its intricate shapes and lustrous glaze, Belleek was invented in the 1860s and almost immediately was a huge success on both sides of the Atlantic. In fact, so great was its popularity that for a period of about 50 years, from the 1880s to around 1930, Belleek was also made in America by a handful of potteries in New Jersey and Ohio

---

Erma Brown lives in a three-story frame house bursting with the Belleek porcelain that she and her husband have collected.

---

whose products rivaled and in some cases surpassed the beauty of the Irish original.

Irish Belleek was the result of a merger between an existing British porcelain, called Parian ware, and a newly developed French glaze *(pages 36-37)*. The porcelain is a warm, creamy white, similar in tone to the Parian marble of ancient Greece; the glaze is iridescent and resembles mother-of-pearl. The first American Belleek, introduced in 1883 by Ott and Brewer of Trenton,

New Jersey, is almost a facsimile of the Irish ware—and no wonder. Three of the key men at the Ott and Brewer works were former employees of the Irish company.

To many collectors, myself included, Ott and Brewer is the finest Belleek ever made in America or anywhere else *(opposite and page 38)*. It is unbelievably light—a dozen Ott and Brewer cups and saucers, 24 pieces in all, weigh only a pound. Understandably, it commands the highest prices. But other early examples of American Belleek, almost as fine and almost as valuable, were made about the same time by other potters in the Trenton area: Willets Manufacturing Company; Morris and Willmore; and Rittenhouse, Evans and Company. Rittenhouse, Evans' Belleek frequently bears the name of its art-pottery operation, American Art China Co.

One of my prize pieces is a Morris and Willmore teapot *(page 41)* offered me by a man who called to say he had a "Belleek chicken" for sale. He tried to describe it over the phone, but the more he talked the more confused I became. Finally I went to his home, and I found a fine, fancy Morris and Willmore teapot that looked more like a dragon than a chicken to me. But I was not about to argue, and I bought it on the spot.

An American Belleek sugar bowl by Willets Manufacturing Company mimics the luster and pattern of an Irish Belleek cup and saucer.

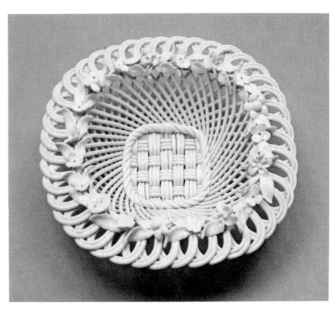

A woven basket of porcelain strands by the American firm Willets is a close copy of a specialty item long identified with Irish Belleek.

One Trenton pottery was set up to manufacture Belleek. Called The Ceramic Art Company and often known simply as CAC, it was formed in 1889 by two former employees of Ott and Brewer, Walter Scott Lenox and Jonathan Coxon. Eventually the name changed to Lenox, Inc. CAC Belleek *(page 39)* is different in appearance from the Irish Belleek that served as a model. It is heavier in body and warmer in tone, often with a pronounced orange cast. In fact, it looks very much like the Lenox china still produced today, though the modern china no longer carries the Belleek name.

Belleek was also made by several potteries in Ohio. Between 1891 and 1896, The Knowles, Taylor & Knowles Co. of East Liverpool, Ohio, turned out a beautiful milk-white porcelain with a velvety glaze that they called Lotus Ware *(page 41)*. There are some collectors who refuse to recognize this ware as Belleek because it is not labeled Belleek. But as far as I am concerned it deserves the name. It is the same thin, delicate china as the original Belleek—and besides, one of the top artisans on the Knowles staff was Joshua Poole, formerly the manager of the Belleek pottery in Ireland.

Just before the Great Depression, other Ohio manufacturers began making Belleek. Two of them, the Coxon Belleek company and the Morgan Belleek China Co., had roots in Trenton. One was run by the two sons of Jonathan Coxon, co-founder of Lenox; the other was started by veteran New Jersey potter William Morgan. Both firms made very fine Belleek and their wares are sought after by collectors. Later 20th Century Belleek tends to be of lesser quality. Into this category fit the china of three companies that made Belleek in the 1940s and 1950s—the Bellmark Pottery Company; Perlee, Incorporated; and the American Beleek Company, spelled with a single L *(page 45)*.

It was Lenox Belleek that my husband and I first collected. Family connections made it natural for us to do so. My husband's great-uncle became the manager of the Lenox plant when Walter Lenox became paralyzed and blind, and in 1920 was made the company president. But our interest in American Belleek broadened, and as we learned more about it we began looking for the earlier, rarer varieties. These were easier to find than they are now. I used to buy things through magazine advertisements, for instance, but nowadays when I answer an ad I am almost always too late.

Most experienced Belleek collectors are specialists. They concentrate on obtaining as many examples as possible of one particular manufacturer or they limit their buying to one specific kind of decoration. Some collectors, for example, look only for the Lenox factory-decorated wares done by such staff artists as Hans and J. Nosek or George and William Morley. Plates decorated by the Morleys with game birds, fish or fruit and flowers

From Old Ireland, the Ancestral Ware

Belleek porcelain gets its name from the town in Northern Ireland called Belleek, where McBirney & Co. began making the delicate translucent ware in 1863. The Irish pottery, now called Belleek Pottery, Ltd., still stands on an island in the Erne River near the sea. Its craftsmen often decorate the ware with marine motifs: shells, coral, sea horses and mermaids. They also use motifs from local plants, such as roses, thistles and shamrocks. Their best-known wares are woven porcelain baskets and plates like the one below.

The marks that distinguish the Belleek product generally include an Irish wolfhound, a harp, a tower and shamrocks with the name Belleek in one ribbon *(page 44)* and, after 1891, the words County Fermanagh, Ireland, in a second ribbon. Until World War II the marks were stamped in black; the plant then closed briefly, and after production resumed, green was used for the marks.

Openwork porcelain of spaghetti-like strands hand-woven over plaster forms is the specialty associated with Irish Belleek.

An Irish Belleek cream pitcher takes the form of a sea shell with a green, coral-branch handle. It dates from before 1891.

The legendary monster called a griffin decorates a Belleek tea set that includes two pots, one a one-cupper only 3 inches high.

A wine cooler is based on a design conceived for Edward, Prince of Wales, who later became Britain's King Edward VII.

An Irish Belleek vase only 12 inches high manages to include in its design two gaping fish as well as applied butterflies and snails.

have sold for as much as $150 apiece. These staff artists signed their names on the decoration. My own particular favorites are the factory-decorated pitchers of Ott and Brewer, which have twig handles and overall intertwining patterns of ferns, grasses and butterflies in raised bronze and gold.

Other people seek the work of professional decorating shops that bought blanks from potteries and decorated the china with monograms or designs ordered by the purchaser. Decorators whose names are often stamped on the bottom of such pieces are Jesse Dean and the W. H. Tatler Decorating Company of Trenton.

One decorator whose work is of interest to Belleek collectors is Mrs. S. S. Frackleton of Milwaukee, Wisconsin. The daughter of a wealthy banker, Mrs. Frackleton went to finishing school in New York, where she learned the then-fashionable hobby of china painting. On her return to Milwaukee, she founded her own pottery, became important in the art-pottery movement (see *Art Pottery* in a separate volume) and organized the National League of Mineral Painters, an association of professional china painters. Mrs. Frackleton noted in her autobiography that she was the only decorator Ott and Brewer would permit to work on their blanks. However, the name of the Southern China Painters' League appears on at least one example of Ott and Brewer Belleek produced after her book appeared, so it seems reason-

able that the pottery also sold Belleek blanks to other china decorators.

Decorating china was in fact a popular pursuit among well-to-do women from the 1880s to World War I, and much hand-decorated Belleek is the product of their labors. Most of the work of these amateurs can be recognized by its crude workmanship and the design, which runs to cabbage roses and large red apples. But some Belleek done by amateurs is as beautiful—and collectible—as the work of professionals *(page 42)*.

The most elaborately decorated Belleek, known as silver overlay, was made by laying sterling silver onto the surface of the porcelain. Scenic designs are the ones most sought after—geese flying in the sunset, windmills in Holland, Chinese laborers at work *(page 43)*. Much of the ware bears the marks of silver companies, indicating that the companies bought the porcelain as blanks and decorated it themselves. Sometimes the mark is stamped on the bottom, as on the silver overlay of Mauser Manufacturing Company and Rockwell Silver Co. But sometimes the silver itself is marked with the company's hallmark; The Gorham Company always stamped its mark, a lion, an anchor and a "G," in this fashion.

Collecting Belleek requires considerable patience and tenacity—and it sometimes involves travel. The logical place to start is in the shops of dealers who specialize in antique porcelain; their names can often be found in the

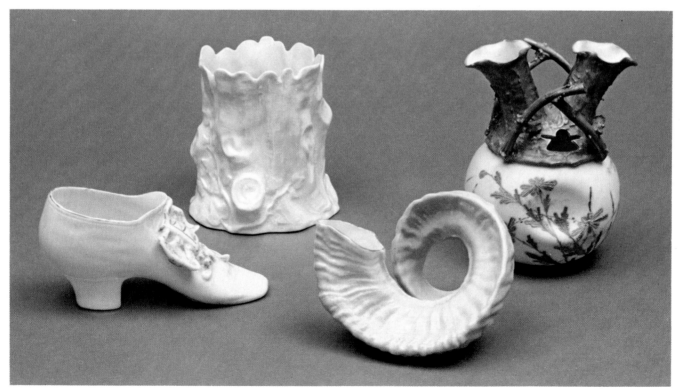

The four unusual curios above, all made by the Ott and Brewer pottery of Trenton, New Jersey, include a ram's-horn vase, a tree- *trunk vase and a twig-handled, double-necked vase (top right). The shoe, a popular Victorian form, was used as a candy dish.*

articles and advertisements of magazines such as *Antiques, Antiques Journal* and *Spinning Wheel.* Dealers in Victoriana of all kinds are also a good source for Belleek. And so are ordinary antique shops in the regions where the Belleek manufacturers were located. Ohiomade Belleek, for example, often turns up in Midwestern antique shops, while Trenton-made Belleek will be easier to find in the Northeast.

My husband and I have scoured the East Coast from Maine to Florida in our hunting, and we have traveled as far west as St. Louis to attend auctions where we knew collections of Belleek were going to be sold. Frequently we hear about such events from other Belleek enthusiasts, who form, I am happy to say, both a widespread and close-knit fraternity, willing to share information with other collectors.

For related material, see the article in this volume on Bennington Pottery, and the articles on Art Pottery, Limoges China, Staffordshire: Figures, Staffordshire: Historic, and Wedgwood in separate volumes of this encyclopedia.

Gilded flowers on a black background decorate a lovely, delicate vase created by The Ceramic Art Company of Trenton.

A porcelain chocolate pot profusely ornamented with fish heads, coral branches and mermaids is another Ceramic Art Company design.

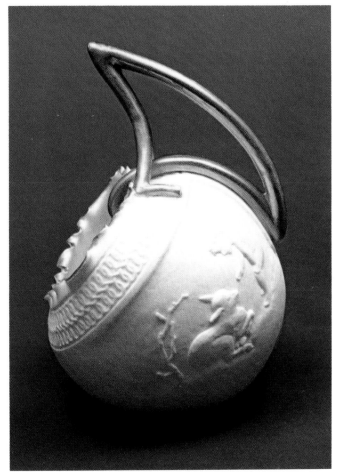

Carvings with a jackknife done before firing by Kate Sears, a decorator for The Ceramic Art Company, make this vase especially rare.

The vaguely Moorish-shaped handles on this American Belleek vase indicate it is from the 1890s, when such decorative devices were popular.

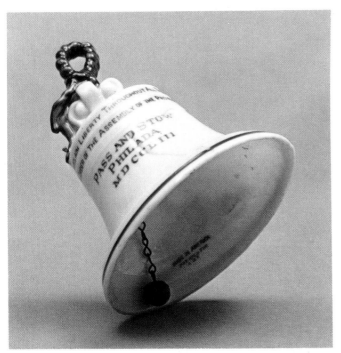

A souvenir bell of Belleek, by Morris and Willmore of Trenton, New Jersey, commemorates the 1893 Columbian Exposition in Chicago.

A teapot in the shape of a ship with a dragon-like figurehead follows a design produced only by Morris and Willmore in the 1890s.

These pieces are Lotus Ware, the trade name for a fine china produced by The Knowles, Taylor and Knowles Company of East Liverpool, Ohio. Lotus Ware is often identified as Belleek because it has the same translucent glow. The pieces above were decorated by Knowles artist Hans Schmidt, who used tools similar to those of cake decorating to create the raised flowers and foliage on the middle vase.

At right is a fruit plate made by Lenox Inc. and prized by collectors for its decoration by company artist William H. Morley. Pieces decorated by W. A. Pickard of Antioch, Illinois, such as the vase below, are also sought after. Below at right are pieces demonstrating amateur and professional decoration. Two amateur vases, at either end, show skill but are not particularly ambitious. The elaborate cameo portrait was done by J. Nosek, a professional china painter.

Belleek beer mugs and pitchers reflect America's growing taste for lager in the last years of the 19th Century. The two mugs at left were made by Lenox; the pitcher by Willets; the mugs at right by The Ceramic Art Company and Morris and Willmore.

A stylized silver overlay depicting Chinese scenes makes this Lenox coffee service from the 1920s a prized item among Belleek collectors. The silver work was seldom done at the pottery, but rather by silversmiths, in this case by Rockwell Silver Co.

BELLEEK MAKERS' MARKS

Since Belleek was made to be treasured, most is marked. Shown here are the marks of major U.S. producers and one mark of the Irish pottery. Some firms altered marks over the years, and Lenox' name appears with those of other firms that decorated some of its blanks. Dates for U.S. marks indicate the years each pottery made Belleek.

McBIRNEY & CO.
(Predecessor, Belleek Pottery)
County Fermanagh, Ireland
Principal mark 1863-1891

OTT AND BREWER
Trenton, New Jersey
1883-1892

WILLETS
MANUFACTURING COMPANY
Trenton, New Jersey
1884-1909

MORRIS AND WILLMORE
Trenton, New Jersey
1893-1900

RITTENHOUSE,
EVANS & CO.
Trenton, New Jersey
1890-1895

AMERICAN ART
CHINA CO.
Trenton, New Jersey
1891-1895

THE CERAMIC ART COMPANY
(Predecessor of Lenox)
Trenton, New Jersey
1889-1896 (left); 1896-1906 (right)

LENOX, INC.
Trenton, New Jersey
1906-1924

THE KNOWLES, TAYLOR &
KNOWLES CO.
East Liverpool, Ohio
1891-1896

COXON BELLEEK
Wooster, Ohio
1926-1930

MORGAN BELLEEK
CHINA CO.
Canton, Ohio
1924-1929

PERLEE, INCORPORATED
Trenton, New Jersey
1922-1930

Much work by lesser-known potteries is quite handsome. Shown here, from left, are a teapot by Perlee, Inc., a plate by Coxon Belleek, a mug by the Bellmark Pottery Company, a Morgan Belleek China Co. tray and an American Beleek Company vase.

Belleek collectors call miniature oil lamps such as the one above sparking lamps, since courting couples used to woo, or "spark," by their fitful glow. This example is 2½ inches high.

MUSEUMS
Museum of Ceramics
East Liverpool, Ohio 43920

New Jersey State Museum
Trenton, New Jersey 08625

COLLECTORS ORGANIZATIONS
Belleek Society International
P.O. Box 266
Houston, Texas 77001

BOOKS
Barber, Edwin Atlee, *The Pottery and Porcelain of the United States and Marks of American Potters.* Feingold and Lewis, 1976. Reprint of 1909 edition.

Hughes, G. Bernard, *Victorian Pottery and Porcelain.* Macmillan, 1959.

Shinn, Charles and Dorrie, *Victorian Parian China.* Barrie & Jenkins, London, 1971.

Bells
Collecting for Sound and Shape

S oon after I started collecting, I began to dream of finding a special cowbell. I wanted one with a sound that was haunting yet peaceful, poignant yet lulling. One evening, while on vacation in North Carolina, I heard the sound I had been waiting for. It came drifting across the night air from a nearby farm. In the morning, my husband went to see if he could buy the bell, but it turned out that the farmer had borrowed it from a friend and could not sell it. On the way home, my husband pulled up at a country store. He and my daughter ordered me to stay in the car while they went inside, leaving me little doubt about the object of their errand. Before long, they came out laughing. They had asked the owner of the store to let them hear every cowbell on his shelves. "My heavens, folks," he

A Japanese horse bell has iron pellet clappers.

Rebecca Mayer of Atlanta has in 30 years acquired more than 400 bells. She is past president of the American Bell Association and founder of Bells in Distress, a group that restores public bells.

---

said, "you must have a large herd of cows." My daughter left him speechless when she replied, "It's not for a cow. It's for my mother."

Of course, you have to expect to be the object of a little ribbing if you have carried on a 30-year love affair with bells. It began when a friend gave me one and challenged me to see how many others I could find. By the end of that year, I had 50; now I have hundreds in every nook of my home. They were used to sound alarms, rejoice in victory, grieve in defeat, hail newlyweds, toll for the dead. They are made of metals—bronze, iron, brass, silver, gold and a copper-and-tin alloy called bell metal—and wood and glass.

Though most of the bells I own were made in modern times, a few accompanied ancient rulers to the grave. Known as crotals, they have been found in tombs of Egyptian pharaohs and Inca kings in Peru. Their form, called closed mouth, is still used for some kinds of bells,

among them the ones that are tied onto Christmas packages. Open-mouth bells are found just about everywhere. The inverted-tulip "bell-shaped" form is most common in the United States and Europe. It is found occasionally in the Far East. But more Oriental bells *(page 54)* are gongs; lacking clappers, they must be struck on the outside.

Among the desirable types are animal bells from Switzerland, prized for musical quality, and porcelain bells from France and Austria, valued for beauty. In other European countries a glazed pottery called faïence is used for bells.

One special type always attracts collectors. This is the nodder, made in the form of a human or animal figure whose head or torso sways as the bell rings *(page 51)*. The trick is simple. What would ordinarily be the handle of the bell is attached to the clapper. The nodder is struck by tapping the handle, and as long as the bell rings, the nodder nods.

There are numbers of reproductions of popular bells, many of poor quality but others so similar to the originals that even experts can be fooled. Special types, such as the faïence called Capo di Monte *(page 51)*, are often imitated, as are bells from the Meissen factory in Germany. Genuine Meissen bears the crossed-swords mark that has been used for two centuries—but so do many spurious pieces. Obviously, age is a factor in value, so much so that fakers go to the trouble of assembling composites—bells made from parts of two or more old bells, or from a genuine old bell and a fake handle. Most composites are brass hand bells, and sometimes the handles are of a brass that matches the bell surprisingly well without any refinishing. As for distinguishing old brass from new, the surface of an older piece has a satin touch and shows the effects of decades of rubbing. The clappers of old metal bells, moreover, were never finely finished. Age has never seemed overwhelmingly important to me, however, and my collection includes many new bells. I like them all.

The air-raid bell at left was used in Britain during World War II. Its surface, now polished, was blackened then for security. The bell above, used around 1880 in England, is from a set mounted in servants' quarters and rung by pulling cords attached to hidden wires. Each bell had its own tone, to indicate the room the summons came from.

A brass ship's bell used aboard an American clipper in the Far East hangs from a bracket adorned with brass dolphins, which symbolize good luck to Western sailors. The dolphin mount seems to have been influenced by similar dragon mounts made for Oriental bells.

Once part of a set of about six matching pieces, this 19th Century French bell was kept on a woman's dressing table to call her maid. Pressure on the bird figurine activates a clapper inside the bell.

This unusual bell-candlestick, solid brass 16 inches high, has been identified as a type of excommunication bell, used to signify expulsion from the Church.

This British figurine bell was used in the 1800s for signaling servants to bring tea.

The bells above, from Europe, are made of
different kinds of glass. From left to right:
yellow-lined pink luster glass with applied
flowers; Italian millefiori, or thousand-
flowers, glass; diamond-quilted art glass;
satin ribbon glass. At right are three French
bells. The one with the bird-shaped handle
was made by famed glassmaker René La-
lique. The others belong to a set of 13 pieces,
each with a different figure on its handle.

These earthenware bells are Italian. The one at left is known as Capo di Monte; the other is of a kind called Spaghetti ware.

The full skirts of these French ceramic figurines are bells; the small bell is by the early-20th Century potter Henri Quimper.

Connected by wire to the clapper inside, the head of this porcelain Staffordshire nodder bobs when the bell is rung. If a nodder is well balanced, a swing of the clapper moves the head for 30 minutes.

This table bell was made in the 18th Century at the Meissen porcelain factory in Germany. It is in the style of Jacob Petit, a French designer who specialized in delicately applied, hand-modeled flowers.

A chime with graduated cups, once worn by camels in Persia, is inscribed with a peacock, an ancient Persian symbol of tolerance.

These brass elephant bells from India are crotals, or closed-mouth bells, that were designed with "tiger-claw" closings for their mouths. The noise of the bell was intended to frighten off the elephant's natural enemy, the Bengal tiger.

This cowbell is of the kind traditionally used by Basque herdsmen in the Pyrenees Mountains between Spain and France. It is made of sheet iron and has a bentwood handle.

A small brass American turkey bell in the foreground is surrounded by bells made for other animals. Clockwise from lower left: brass and iron sheep bells and cowbells from New England, a wooden bullock bell from Thailand, an iron cowbell from Austria with a Tyrolean mountain scene and a closed-mouth Belgian horse bell with the form of a horse in relief.

Called a parade flier and designed to be mounted on a horse's collar, this contraption was made in America around the 1790s. Two bells with different tones swing under horsehair plumes. A third bell, motionless under the eagle figurine, is rung by moving clappers.

The song "Jingle Bells" was inspired by bells like these, fastened—usually in various sizes—to bellybands worn by horses pulling sleighs.

This ancient bronze Japanese wind chime is sometimes called a snail bell because its nine protuberances are thought to symbolize the Buddhist legend of sacred snails that cooled Buddha's head in the desert.

One side of this iron bell from Kenya, used for casting spells, was made longer than the other so that the bell would give two tones.

Two figures stand back to back on the handle of a Hindu evolution bell, so called because the figures represent two gods who gave birth to another. Visible above is the monkey nymph Anjana; behind it is the wind god Vayu. Their offspring was the holy monkey Hanuman.

This Roman Catholic Sanctus bell, sometimes called a sacristy bell, is sculptured to resemble a large tree branch, with four smaller branches holding bells and supporting bird figurines. The bells represent the four gospels and the birds represent the harmony of the gospels.

Storks, whose feathers were said to have lined Christ's manger, are inscribed on this bronze baptism bell, often called a stork bell.

MUSEUMS
Virginia Brewer Bell Museum
Canton, Texas 75103

Elliott Bell Museum
Tarentum, Pennsylvania 15084

Stephen Foster Center
White Springs, Florida 32096

Winston Jones Bell Museum
Evergreen, Colorado 80439

Margaret Woodbury Strong Museum
Rochester, New York 14618

COLLECTORS ORGANIZATIONS
The American Bell Association
R.D. 1, Box 286
Natrona Heights, Pennsylvania 15065

PERIODICALS
The Bell Tower. The American Bell Association,
Natrona Heights, Pennsylvania 15065

BOOKS
Anthony, Dorothy Malone:
The World of Bells, No. 1. Wallace-Homestead
Book Company, 1971.
The World of Bells, No. 2. Wallace-Homestead
Book Company, 1974.
The World of Bells, No. 3. Wallace-Homestead
Book Company, 1977.

Coleman, Satis N., *Bells: Their History,
Legends, Making, and Uses*. Gale Research Company,
1971.

Morris, Ernest:
Bells of All Nations. Robert Hale, Ltd.,
1951.
*History and Art of Change Ringing: The Definitive
Art of Bell Ringing*. Beekman Publications, Inc.,
1975.
Tintinnabula. Robert Hale, Ltd., 1959.
Towers and Bells of Britain. Robert Hale, Ltd.,
1955.

Sloane, Eric, *The Sound of Bells*. Doubleday and
Company, 1966.

Springer, L. Elsinore:
The Collector's Book of Bells. Crown Publishers, Inc.,
1972.
That Vanishing Sound. Crown Publishers, Inc.,
1976.

Tyack, G. S., *A Book About Bells*. Aryphon Press,
1971.

Fenton's
ENAMEL.
PATENTED
1849
PENNINGTON.

Bennington Pottery
One Visionary's Artful Creations

All the normal criteria for locating a pottery make Bennington, Vermont, an unlikely choice for a site. It is, after all, a small town snuggled among the mountains of southern Vermont, miles from markets and any major pottery centers. Although clay can be found locally, it is not all of the best quality. During the 19th Century, when Bennington's potteries flourished, raw materials had to be brought in—and the finished products shipped out—over poorly maintained dirt roads. Yet some of the most beautifully crafted pottery produced in the United States was made there.

There were two separate pottery operations in Bennington, but only one was involved in the creation of

---

Robert B. Condon, a motel owner in Bennington, Vermont, has been collecting wares from the long-defunct local potteries since 1963. His collection includes more than 100 examples.

---

what collectors generally call Bennington pottery. The first, established by Connecticut-born Captain John Norton in 1793, ran a calm and predictable course for a total of 101 years, turning out utilitarian jugs and crocks. At first it produced redware, a soft ceramic of brick clay dug nearby; then it turned to harder, longer-lasting stoneware made of clay barged up the Hudson River and carted overland to Vermont.

The other pottery lasted fewer than 20 years, marked by abrupt changes of direction and ambitious efforts at innovation. When collectors speak of Bennington ware, it is mainly the output of this second operation, guided by an erratic character named Christopher Webber Fenton, that they have in mind. Fenton came to Bennington from Dorset, Vermont, where his family made pottery, and he married into the Norton family. He was made a partner in the Norton firm, but dreamed of extending its operation beyond everyday stoneware, and in 1847 struck out on his own, at first in an unoccupied portion of the Norton works.

The new concern, Fenton's Works, later to be known as Lyman, Fenton & Co. and then as the United States

A patent mark stamped into a piece of Bennington pottery is dated 1849, the year Christopher Webber Fenton patented Flint Enamel.

Pottery Company, experienced an astonishingly rapid expansion. In 1850 a massive three-oven pottery was built and soon afterward a well-known English pottery designer, Daniel Greatbach, was hired. He is credited with the design of the pottery's animal forms—poodles, lions, cows, deer—as well as bottles and pitchers in the familiar "Toby jug" style. He also created the famous Bennington hound-handled pitcher, whose handle resembles the head and body of a dog *(page 58)*.

The most sought-after Fenton products include pottery with a mottled-brown, glazed finish called Rockingham *(opposite)*, after the Rockingham Potteries in England, where it was first developed. Rockingham was made in more than 100 potteries in the U.S. and other countries. At first, while in partnership with Norton, Fenton made Rockingham that was almost uniform in color. He dipped his pieces into a glaze bath of manganese to obtain a lustrous brown finish and called the result "Dark Luster Ware." Pitchers from this period are rather rare. Later Fenton developed techniques for unusual mottling effects; it is this splotched, two-tone ware that most people associate with Bennington pottery.

For his mottled Rockingham, Fenton first applied a glossy underglaze to the fired ware. Then he dipped a paddle into the manganese glaze and struck the paddle on the vat's edge so that drops of glaze spattered the pottery as it rotated. On the second firing this process created a streaked glaze, with some areas more heavily spattered than others. At thin spots the yellow body clay showed through, creating a tortoise-shell effect.

In 1849 Fenton patented another mottling method called Flint Enamel. Over a clear glaze, still wet, the potter sprinkled powdered oxides that produced various colors—oxides of cobalt for blue, of manganese for brown, of copper for green. When the piece was fired, the oxides melted and ran together, creating a streaked, multicolored effect. A different process produced the prized scroddled ware *(page 65)*. Clays of various hues were mixed so that bands of color ran throughout the piece, making it look a bit like marble cake.

Fenton's real passion, however, was porcelain, the hard, translucent ceramic ware made of the clay known as kaolin. Much Bennington porcelain was Parian, an unglazed ware resembling white marble in color and

Dogs peer over the rims of two "hound-handled" pitchers, but only the smaller is true Bennington; the green mat color of the other indicates that it was made in Tiltonsville, Ohio, from a Bennington mold.

texture, and named for the Aegean island where the Greeks quarried marble. Developed in England, Parian was first produced in America by Fenton, who used it to make small figurines, ewers and vases with applied decorations such as grapes, leaves and tendrils.

Fenton became a major American source of high-quality ceramics, but had many problems. The biggest was shipping: the fine wares were fragile. Most had to be shipped by horse and wagon, and breakage was extensive. Fenton also had trouble collecting payments.

Such difficulties might have been surmounted by a steadier personality, but it appears that Fenton was somewhat volatile and capricious. In *The Potters and Potteries of Bennington,* John Spargo describes him as "being easily angered in discussion, rather uncertain in his relations with his men, restless in manner . . . constantly altering plans and orders." Fenton was also "addicted to constant dram-drinking intensified by periodic 'sprees' followed by mental depression and despondency." In 1858 the pottery went bankrupt, and, although sporadic attempts were made to revitalize the business, most collectors consider the wares made after

1858 to be inferior. Fenton himself worked briefly in a pottery in South Carolina, then founded a short-lived pottery in Peoria, Illinois, where he died in 1865.

Of all of Fenton's output, I have a special fondness for his Flint Enamel because this got me into collecting. One day in 1963 I saw a Flint Enamel cuspidor at an antique show in Bennington. A mark on the bottom indicated that it had been made in 1849. I telephoned a nearby collector friend to ask him whether the piece was a good buy. He was intrigued by my question and said, "I'll be right down." "Oh, no," I said, "this one's for me," and I went right back and bought the cuspidor.

A great deal of Flint Enamel was made in Bennington: pie plates, small pots called pipkins, picture frames, vases, bowls, pitchers, soap dishes, chamber pots, doorknobs and curtain tiebacks. Flint Enamel was also used for lion figurines *(page 66),* and cream pitchers in the shape of cows and Toby jugs. But Flint Enamel is so popular among collectors that fine pieces are scarce. Perhaps the rarest flint pieces are lamp bases *(page 60);* fewer than a dozen are known to exist.

Fenton seems to have made little scroddled ware—it

A sugar bowl reveals the unusual mottling achieved by Christopher Webber Fenton in his spattering technique for Flint Enamel.

This pitcher's shape and uniform glaze mark it as a rare example of the Rockingham ware Fenton produced early in his career.

was not popular in its time—and this unusual marble-ized pottery is difficult to find today. It also appears to be more brittle than Fenton's other wares; certainly it is hard to find an example without a crack or chip. But an avid collector can occasionally locate a bowl and pitcher set in reasonably good condition, or a cuspidor or a "book flask"—a whiskey bottle in the shape of a book.

Fenton was more successful with white earthenware than he was with scroddled ware, and a great deal more of it has survived. He used it for a variety of tableware, some of which was decorated with gold before glazing. Pieces resembling human or animal figures made in tougher white earthenware called graniteware were also popular and are therefore common today. Unglazed Parian porcelain, too, is fairly easy to find.

When buying Parian—or any of Fenton's products—you have to be careful about identification. Only about 20 per cent of Fenton's porcelain was marked, and it was often modeled after English forms. I have two pitchers *(page 62)*, one Bennington, one English, that look so much alike you have to put them side by side to see the difference. Many other types of popular Bennington

pottery, such as Tobys and hound-handled pitchers, were also made elsewhere. Only after study and observation can you distinguish unmarked Fenton pieces.

You can count on two identification aids. Since most Bennington ware was made in molds, it is possible to find unmarked pieces that precisely match marked examples—and may thus be attributed with some confidence to Fenton's pottery. The second aid is Richard Carter Barret's book, *Bennington Pottery and Porcelain*, which illustrates and describes most of the types known.

Bennington is often expensive, especially if it is in good condition. Not surprisingly, marked pieces are the hardest to find and cost the most. But you may be lucky on occasion. I was when I bought a small blue-and-white porcelain pitcher. I could not find it in Barret's book. But at the Bennington Museum I found a larger specimen in the identical pattern. I had come across a rare variant—just the sort of find every collector yearns for.

For related material, see the article in this volume on Belleek Porcelain, and the articles on Art Pottery, Folk Pottery, Majolica, Staffordshire and Toby Mugs in separate volumes.

A Flint Enamel coffeepot glows with the rich colors that come from a glaze permeated with several metallic oxides.

A rare lamp has a base of Fenton's Flint Enamel with a globe and hanging prisms of glass, probably from Sandwich, Massachusetts.

Flint Enamel cuspidors are among the more plentiful Bennington, perhaps because collectors consider them useless and vulgar.

Flint Enamel pie plates were produced at Bennington in great quantity, but pipkins—bean pots—are rare and especially hard to find with the fragile handles still intact.

A giant Flint Enamel mixing bowl, nearly 2 feet in diameter, and a miniature bowl and pitcher set less than 4 inches high exemplify *common Bennington forms in uncommon sizes. The pottery produced many different types of miniatures as novelties.*

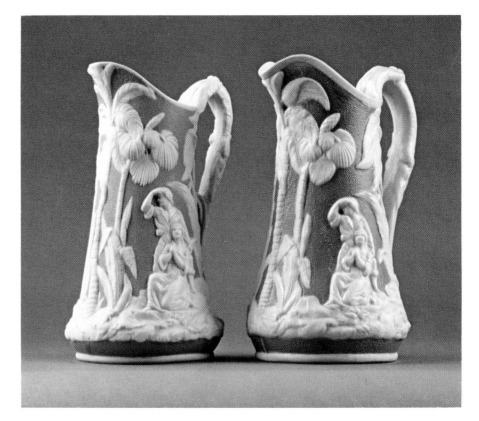

Aside from color variation, a British-made pitcher (left) looks identical to a Bennington design, but subtle differences are perceptible. The lips of the pitchers are contoured differently, the uppermost palm leaf is larger on the Bennington piece and a small spot of color is visible on the British pitcher between the top of the design and the rim.

Sheaf-of-wheat pitchers that Fenton executed in blue and green graniteware—a type of earthenware—are hard to find, because he made few copies in these experimental colors and never marked them. Fenton also produced this design in light gray and white.

This "sweetheart" pitcher of gold-decorated earthenware bears the name of the lady for whom it was made.

Marks on Bennington Pottery

The business methods employed by Christopher Webber Fenton, the eccentric master potter of Bennington, Vermont, were sometimes governed more by whim than by logic. Certainly consistency was not one of his virtues when it came to marking his pottery. Less than a quarter of it bears any mark at all, and the marks he used varied over time as Fenton formed various partnerships and patented new glazes.

These varied marks, if confusing, can also sometimes be of help to the collector, since they aid in dating Fenton's pieces. Fenton's first partnership was with the older Bennington pottery firm, founded and run by the Norton family. The stormy Norton-Fenton alliance lasted from 1845 to 1847. Pottery produced in that brief period is marked "Norton & Fenton, East Bennington Vt.," or "Norton & Fenton, Bennington Vt."

From 1847 until 1849 Fenton's mark read "Fenton's Works, Bennington, Vermont." Fenton next formed a partnership with Alanson Potter Lyman and, by 1849, had patented his Flint Enamel process. So the firm's name and the 1849 date appear in various forms on some work done between 1849 and 1858:

Lyman, Fenton & Co. Fenton's Enamel Patented 1849 Bennington, Vt.
Fenton's Patent Enamel 1849 Lyman, Fenton & Co.
Fenton's Enamel 1849 Patented
Fenton's Enamel Patented 1849 Lyman, Fenton & Co. Bennington, Vt.

Marks used mainly on porcelains and scroddled ware between 1853, when Fenton again changed the firm's name, and 1858, when the firm failed, contain the words "United States Pottery Co. Bennington, Vt." or the initials "U.S.P." in one of two designs, a ribbon or an oval.

This porcelain vase with a green glaze under the applied decoration is rare because Fenton customarily employed blue to color porcelain.

A graceful swan decorates a vase molded from the porcelain called Parian, which, when left uncolored, resembles white marble.

Bennington trinket boxes and cologne bottles of molded Parian porcelain are all unmarked. If the bottle still had its stopper it would be even more valuable.

Parian "pond lily" pitchers were made in various heights; this one is 9¾ inches tall.

A Bennington washbowl and pitcher set, which was manufactured between 1853 and 1858, is of Fenton's desirable marbled scroddled ware. The sides of the pitcher and bowl bear the diamond pattern that also was used for Bennington Flint Enamel and Rockingham wares.

The lion, glazed with Flint Enamel, is one of the popular kinds of animal figurines produced by Fenton's pottery. Collectors also search for figurines of cows (bottom), dogs and deer, all of which were produced in both Flint Enamel and Rockingham glazes.

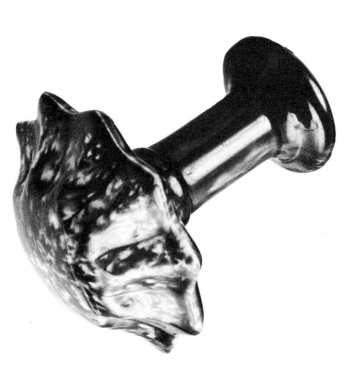

Modest household items produced in Bennington include curtain tiebacks like the one above, finished in Flint Enamel glaze.

Book-shaped flasks were made of scroddled ware (center, above) or finished with Rockingham (right) or Flint Enamel glaze.

Two Bennington pottery collectors of today smile from a Flint Enamel picture frame made by Fenton's works more than a century ago.

MUSEUMS
Bennington Museum
Bennington, Vermont 05201

The Brooklyn Museum
Brooklyn, New York 11238

Greenfield Village and Henry Ford Museum
Dearborn, Michigan 48124

The New-York Historical Society
New York, New York 10024

BOOKS
Barret, Richard Carter:
Bennington Pottery and Porcelain. Crown Publishers, 1958.
How to Identify Bennington Pottery. The Stephen Greene Press, 1964.

Ketchum, William C., Jr., *The Pottery and Porcelain Collector's Handbook: A Guide to Early American Ceramics from Maine to California.* Funk & Wagnalls, 1971.

Spargo, John, *The Potters and Potteries of Bennington.* Cracker Barrel Press, 1926.

Watkins, Lura Woodside, *Early New England Potters and Their Wares.* Harvard University Press, 1950.

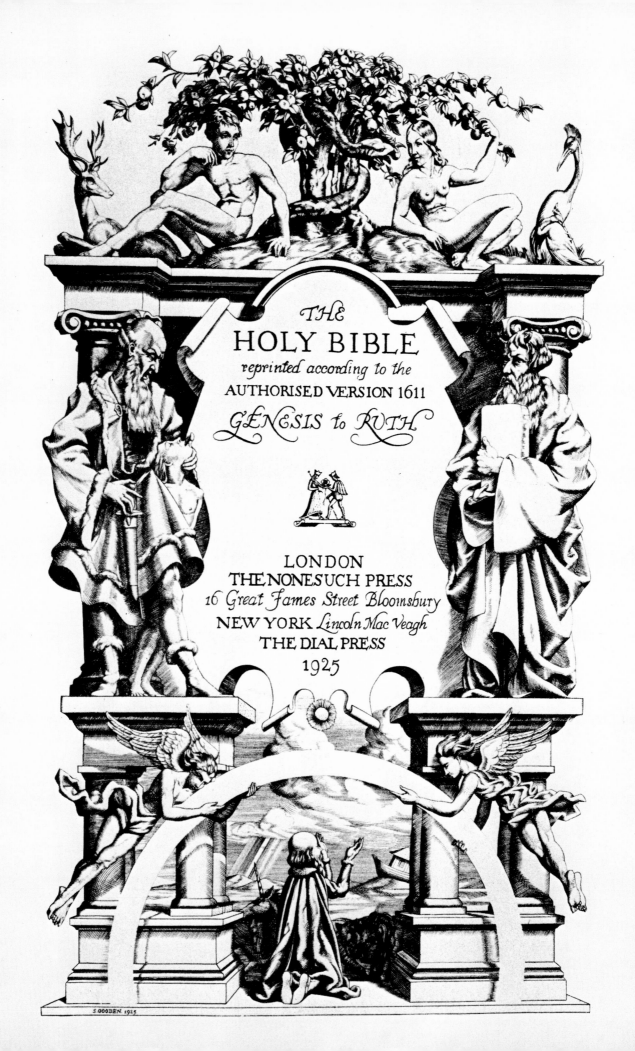

THE
HOLY BIBLE
reprinted according to the
AUTHORISED VERSION 1611
GENESIS to RUTH

LONDON
THE NONESUCH PRESS
16 Great James Street Bloomsbury
NEW YORK Lincoln Mac Veagh
THE DIAL PRESS
1925

S. GOODEN. 1925.

Bibles
Antiquities, Art, Curiosities

The Bible was the first book ever printed—by Johann Gutenberg at Mainz, Germany, about 1455—and since then the Holy Scriptures have been printed in more editions and in greater numbers than any other work. According to one count, in the United States alone, 2,573 editions of Holy Writ were published in the 180 years between 1777 and 1957; millions of copies of these many editions survive today. Bibles range in value from the rare Gutenberg to those mass-produced hotel-room Bibles that have relatively little monetary worth. Only 48 Gutenberg copies are known to exist, and one put on sale in 1970 was priced at $2.5 million (nearly a decade later it remained unsold).

While a Gutenberg Bible is beyond the reach of anyone but the curator of a well-endowed museum, many collectors can own a part of one. The reason is that in

Ben R. Donaldson, originally a schoolteacher but for many years advertising director of the Ford Motor Company, has a collection of more than 1,000 Bibles, plus early manuscripts and prayer books.

1921 an incomplete copy of the Gutenberg Bible was broken up by bookseller Gabriel Wells and sold one leaf at a time. These leaves are resold occasionally at auctions, generally bringing $3,000 or $4,000 for a "very good" leaf—one that contains a famous passage such as the Twenty-third Psalm or the Ten Commandments. There is less demand for the Old Testament chapters that consist primarily of genealogies, "the begats," as they have come to be known.

Since Bibles are so numerous, most collectors are selective in building up a group of volumes. Some people have specialized in miniature Bibles, tiny pocket Gospels about 4 inches high or less. Others have collected Bibles whose text has been translated into American Indian languages such as Cree, Cherokee, Algonquin or Chippewa. Still other collectors have sought beautiful modern Bibles published by small presses that specialize in fine type, illustrations and binding. Those with a title

The title page of the five-volume Nonesuch Press Bible shows the elegant illustration and typography that make this modern edition of the King James translation of 1611 a prize for collectors.

page crediting such highly regarded private presses as Ashendene, Doves, Nonesuch or Corvinus are desirable.

Yet other collectors have been known to acquire only "nickname" Bibles—editions that have gained often comical nicknames because they contain bizarre misprints or variants on standard text. And some seek Bibles that were owned by famous people.

Many Bible collectors, like other collectors of books *(pages 92-117)*, hunt "firsts"—first editions of notable versions of the Bible, or the first Bible printed in a particular place: England, America, Rome, London, Boston. I have been fortunate enough to acquire several firsts. My collection includes the first illustrated Bible, the first complete Bible printed in English, the first in German and the first Roman Catholic edition in English, called the Rheims-Douay for the two French towns where it had to be printed during the fiercely Protestant reigns of Queen Elizabeth I and James I.

For Americans, probably the most important Bible is the Aitken Bible, published in Philadelphia in 1782. The Aitken was the first Bible printed in this country in English. The English Crown had earlier reserved the right to print all English-language Bibles for use in the Colonies. Bibles could be printed in the Colonies in other languages, however, and the Aitken Bible was preceded by John Eliot's translation into the Natick Indian language, published in Cambridge, Massachusetts, in 1663, and several Bibles in German printed in Germantown, Pennsylvania, from 1743 on.

Another notable American first is the Julia E. Smith Bible of 1876, the first complete Bible translated by a woman. (Julia Smith, a native of Connecticut, was an advocate of women's rights and refused to pay taxes without having the right to vote. A long legal battle ended when her dairy cows were seized for back taxes.)

These notable firsts and nickname Bibles, as well as many others, are listed in a scholarly book—only 53 pages—called *Rare Bibles*, by Edwin A. Rumball-Petre.

Collecting famous firsts and other rare Bibles can be a costly pursuit. There is a less ambitious area of collecting, however, that lies wide open—the world of 19th Century American Bibles. Among the thousands of different editions, many are fascinating examples of

So rare are Gutenberg Bibles that collectors cherish single leaves, such as this one containing the last verses of the Book of Ezekiel. This leaf was taken from an incomplete volume and sold individually.

changing styles in publishing and of the features that attracted pious Americans of another era—such as the specially provided blank pages for keeping family records. These 19th Century Bibles are staples in flea markets, at auctions, in the back rooms of bookdealers—and in the family attic. Even the most impressive multi-volume sets will not cost a great deal.

One fascinating aspect of collecting 19th Century Bibles is finding Scriptures printed in unlikely places. Hundreds of editions were produced in small towns by obscure printers. Eleven towns in New Hampshire, several in Vermont and 24 in Massachusetts published editions of Scriptures. Bibles were published in 20 New York towns, 10 towns in New Jersey and 13 in Pennsylvania. Bible publishing also went south and west to places like Buffaloe, Virginia, and Xenia, Ohio.

Dozens of special editions of Scriptures were prepared and published for various religious denominations. The Rheims-Douay Roman Catholic Bible went through many printings, the first in 1790. There were Baptist Bibles and Unitarian Bibles, which altered the traditional New Testament text to reflect the Unitarian skepticism about Christ's divinity. A bowdlerized Bible was produced by Noah Webster, the dictionary maker, who removed words from the sacred texts that were, he said, offensive to delicacy. There is a Bible translated into Komstok's Purfekt Alfabet by one Andrew Comstock, M.D., who was intent on reforming English spelling (evidently including that of his own name). Ten editions of the Scriptures were printed in the Confederacy during the Civil War and thousands of pocket-sized Gospels were produced for the Union troops.

Aside from these fascinating oddities, the collector of American Bibles may wish to acquire some of the fine scholarly editions of the Good Book produced throughout the 19th Century. A leading example is the edition commonly called the Scott Family Bible. This bulky work—it was usually published in five large volumes—was named for an English clergyman, Thomas Scott, who wrote a "copious" commentary that explains every verse of the Old and New Testaments. Scott's Bible, first published between 1804 and 1809 and sold (like many old Bibles) by subscription, was a favorite of Thomas Jefferson's and went through many editions.

American Bibles of both the 19th and 20th centuries have led the way in Biblical illustration. In the early years illustrations were often woodcuts or engravings that copied famous European religious paintings. Later, some editions were illustrated by American artists whose interpretations of Bible scenes were on occasion original and imaginative. By 1843 Harper and Brothers of New York had produced an "Illuminated Bible" with 1,600 small engravings. From 1870, many family Bibles included pictures by the famous illustrator, Gustave Doré.

A number of American Bibles are notable for their typographic devices. Some have the words of Jesus printed in red or in bold italics. Others have stars in the margins opposite Old Testament prophesies that came true in the New Testament.

When a collector of 19th Century Bibles finds a volume from a small Vermont town, say, or an edition with interesting commentary, or a copy recording in old-fashioned handwriting the milestone dates of a notable family, he should consult Margaret Hill's bibliography, *The English Bible in America (page 21),* to ascertain exactly what he has discovered. He might also look at Rumball-Petre's list of 48 important and rare American editions of Scriptures. There is hardly any chance of stumbling across a Gutenberg in an American attic, but prize copies of the more than 2,500 editions of the Bible printed in the United States over the past two centuries must be spread across the country, forgotten for decades and waiting for sharp eyes to pick them out.

Modern editions of the Bible above include the Revised Standard Version—the widely accepted 1952 translation (middle row, center) *—and the two-volume Bible Designed To Be Read As Literature (bottom row), the King James version edited into modern English.*

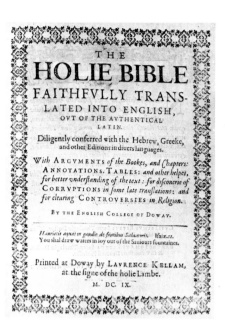

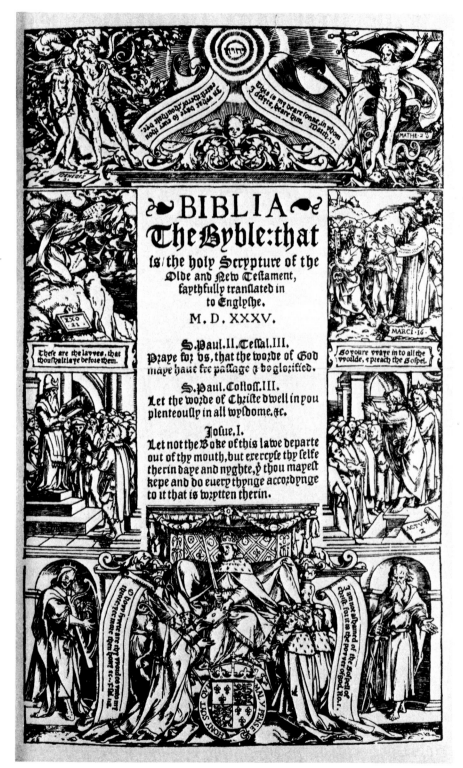

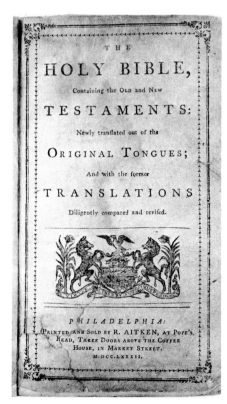

Title pages of important first editions of the Bible in English are reproduced above. On the left is the first complete English Bible, translated from Latin and German texts by Miles Coverdale and published in 1535. At top right is the title page of the Rheims-Douay Bible, the first translation intended for Roman Catholics. At bottom right is the Aitken Bible, the first English Bible printed in America.

THE HOLY
BIBLE
Containing the Bookes
of the Old & New
TESTAMENT
CAMBRIDGE
Printed by John Field
Printer to the Universitie
And illustrated w Chorogra-
phical Sculps by J. Ogilby.
1660.

The elaborately engraved title page of an early illustrated English Bible from 1660 pictures King Solomon surrounded by other Biblical figures.

Sequuntur septem psalmi penitentiales.
Antiphona. Ne reminiscaris. Psalmus.

Artistry of the Medieval Scribes

R arer and more valuable than printed Bibles are those handwritten copies of Holy Writ that were prepared—mostly by scribes in monasteries—before Gutenberg printed the first copy of Scriptures (and the first book) in 1455. Many of these manuscripts are astonishingly beautiful.

Most manuscripts were commissioned by men of wealth and power—princes or high-ranking prelates of the Church—and they wanted their books to look rich and magnificent. The scribes were challenged by such commissions, since the labor involved in copying a work as long as the Bible, which contains almost 800,000 words, was a long and tedious task.

As a result, the manuscripts were enriched—that is, illuminated—with detailed pictures and elaborate initial letters, such as those shown here. Some pages glowed with gold paint. Others came alive with miniatures, a word originally derived from *minium,* the red pigment frequently used by the artists who drew the pictures. In an age when only a few people could read, miniatures not only were decorative, but they also helped convey a religious message.

In addition to the Scriptures, illuminated manuscripts include Books of Hours, which contain prayers meant to be said at various hours of the day. Some, such as the one done for France's Duc de Berry in the early 15th Century, contain some of the finest art of medieval times.

The vibrant battle scene at left, a miniature from a 16th Century Book of Hours, illustrates the verse, "Except you will be converted, he will brandish his sword," from the Seventh Psalm. Gold initial letters (right) illuminate a 13th Century Latin Bible copied by a scribe in Cambridge, England. The marginal notes explain this passage from the Gospel of St. Mark.

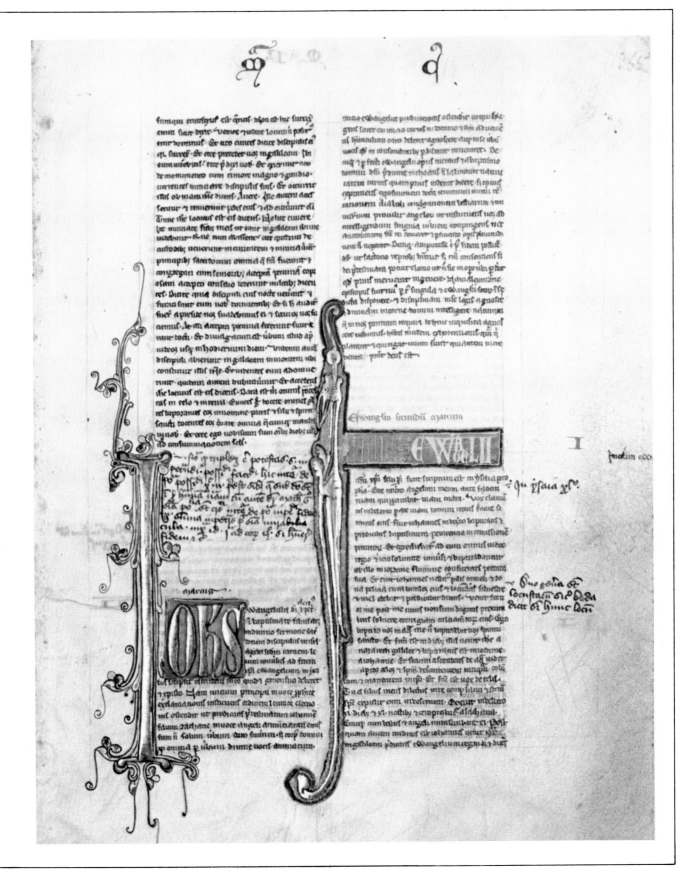

These bindings show the care lavished on religious works. The 1646 Bible (right) has an embroidered, gem-studded binding. The 1634

Book of Common Prayer (left) is embroidered with a picture of King David. The modern Bible (middle) has an engraved silver binding.

A watercolor of the Nativity can be seen when the pages of the prayer book above are fanned backward. This curious method of decorating is called fore-edge painting and was practiced primarily in England

during the 18th and 19th centuries—although the method is still occasionally employed today. The painting above is dated 1890 and is signed by the English artist, John T. Beer.

6 And the woman will see that the tree is good for food, and that it is a desire to the eyes, and a tree desired to make wise; and she will take from its fruit and will eat, and will give also to her man with her, and he will eat.

7 And the eyes of the two shall be opened, and they shall know that they are naked; and they shall sew together the leaves of the fig tree, and shall make to themselves girdles.

Adam and Eve are modestly dressed in girdles of fig leaves in the Bible translated in the 1870s by an American, Julia E. Smith, the first woman to translate the Bible into a modern language.

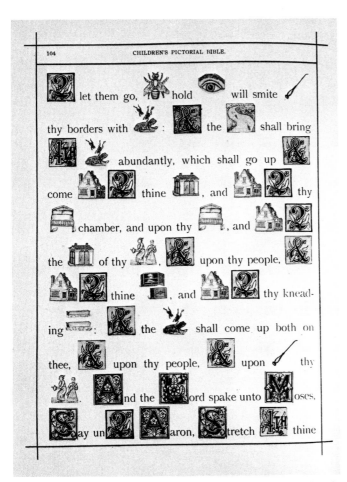

A sought-after oddity is this child's Bible, published in Connecticut in 1830, that substitutes pictures for various words. Called rebus paraphrases, the texts were in vogue in the early 19th Century.

when she helde it, he measured sixe measures of barley, and laide it on her: and he went into the citie.

16 And when shee came to her mother in law, she said, Who art thou, my daughter? and she tolde her all that the man had done to her.

17 And she said, These sixe measures of barley gaue he me, for he said to me, Go not emptie vnto thy mother in law.

A famous "nickname" Bible is the first pressrun of the 1611 King James, in which the Book of Ruth reads, "he went into the citie" instead of "she went." Collectors call this issue the "Great He Bible."

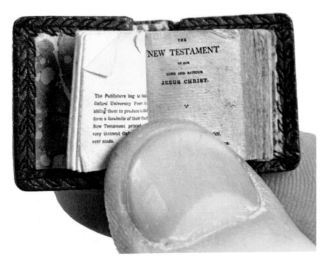

A miniature New Testament printed in Scotland in 1895 is less than ¼ inch thick and ¾ inch high but contains the whole text in 520 pages. Such miniatures are not expensive.

⁎Gen.2.3.   11 For⁎in six dayes the LORD made heauen and earth, the sea and all that in them is, and rested the seuenth day, wherefore the LORD blessed the Sabbath day, and hallowed it.
⁎Deut.5.   12 ¶⁎Honour thy father and thy mother, that
16.mat.   thy dayes may bee long vpon the land which the
15.4.   LORD thy God giueth thee.
ephe 6.2.   13 ⁎ Thou shalt not kill.
⁎ Matth.   14 Thou shalt commit adultery.
5.21.   15 Thou shalt not steale.
   16 Thou shalt not beare false witnesse against thy neighbour.
⁎ Rom.   17 ⁎ Thou shalt not couet thy nighbours house,
7.7.   thou shalt not couet thy neighbours wife, nor his man-seruant, nor his maid-seruant, nor his oxe, nor his asse, nor any thing that is thy neighbours.
⁎ Hebr.   18 ¶ And ⁎ all the people saw the thunderings

The "Wicked Bible" of 1632 mistakenly adjures the faithful, "Thou shalt commit adultery." The employers of the forgetful printers who left out "not" were fined 300 pounds by the British Crown.

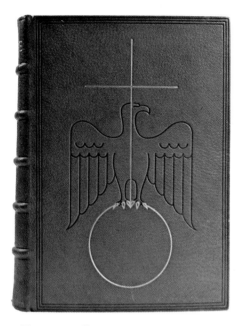

THE
HOLY BIBLE
Containing the Old and New
Testaments : Translated out
of the Original Tongues and
with the former Translations
diligently compared and revised by His Majesty's special
Command

Appointed to be read in Churches

OXFORD
Printed at the University Press
1935

THE REVELATION OF
St. John the Divine

CHAPTER 1

THE Revelation of Jesus Christ, which God gave unto him, to shew unto his servants things which must shortly come to pass; and he sent and signified it by his angel unto his servant John: ¶2 Who bare record of the word of God, and of the testimony of Jesus Christ, and of all things that he saw. ¶3 Blessed is he that readeth, and they that hear the words of this prophecy, and keep those things which are written therein: for the time is at hand. ¶4 JOHN to the seven churches which are in Asia: Grace be unto you, and peace, from him which is, and which was, and which is to come; and from the seven Spirits which are before his throne; ¶5 And from Jesus Christ, who is the faithful witness, and the first begotten of the dead, and the prince of the kings of the earth. Unto him that loved us, and washed us from our sins in his own blood, ¶6 And hath made us kings and priests unto God and his Father; to him be glory and dominion for ever and ever. Amen. ¶7 Behold, he cometh with clouds; and every eye shall see him, and they also which pierced him: and all kindreds of the earth shall wail because of him. Even so, Amen. ¶8 I am Alpha and Omega, the beginning and the ending, saith the Lord, which is, and which was, and which is to come, the Almighty. ¶9 I John, who also am your brother, and companion in tribulation, and in the kingdom and patience of Jesus Christ, was in the isle that is called Patmos, for the word of God, and for the testimony of Jesus Christ. ¶10 I was in the Spirit on the Lord's day, and heard behind me a great voice, as of a trumpet, ¶11 Saying, I am Alpha and Omega, the first and the last: and, What thou seest, write in a book, and send it unto the seven churches which are in Asia; unto Ephesus, and unto Smyrna, and unto Pergamos, and unto Thyatira, and unto Sardis, and unto Philadelphia, and unto Laodicea. ¶12 And I turned to see the voice that spake with me. And being turned, I saw seven golden candlesticks; ¶13 And in the midst of the seven candlesticks one like unto the Son of man, clothed with a garment down to the foot, and girt about the paps with a golden girdle. ¶14 His head and his hairs were white like wool, as white as snow; and his eyes were as a flame of fire; ¶15 And his feet like unto fine brass, as if they burned in a furnace; and his voice as the sound of many waters. ¶16 And he had in his right hand seven stars: and out of his mouth went a sharp two-edged sword: and his countenance was as the sun shineth in his strength. ¶17 And when I saw him, I fell at his feet as dead. And he laid his right hand upon me, saying unto me, Fear not; I am the first and the last: ¶18 I am he that liveth, and was dead; and, behold, I am alive for evermore, Amen; and have the keys of hell and of death. ¶19 Write the things which thou hast seen, and the things which are, and the things which shall be hereafter; ¶20 The mystery of the seven stars which thou sawest in my right hand, and the seven golden candlesticks. The seven stars are the angels of the seven churches: and the seven candlesticks which thou sawest are the seven churches.

CHAPTER 2

UNTO the angel of the church of Ephesus write; These things saith he that holdeth the seven stars in his right hand, who walketh in the midst of the seven golden candlesticks; ¶2 I know thy works, and thy labour, and thy patience, and how thou canst not bear them which are evil: and thou hast tried them which say they are apostles, and are not, and hast found them liars: ¶3 And hast borne, and hast patience, and for my name's sake hast laboured, and hast not fainted. ¶4 Nevertheless

1203

To many collectors, the most beautiful Bible printed in the 20th Century is the 1935 Oxford Press edition, designed by American typographer Bruce Rogers. Above, left to right, are the brown leather binding stamped in gold, the title page and a typical text page.

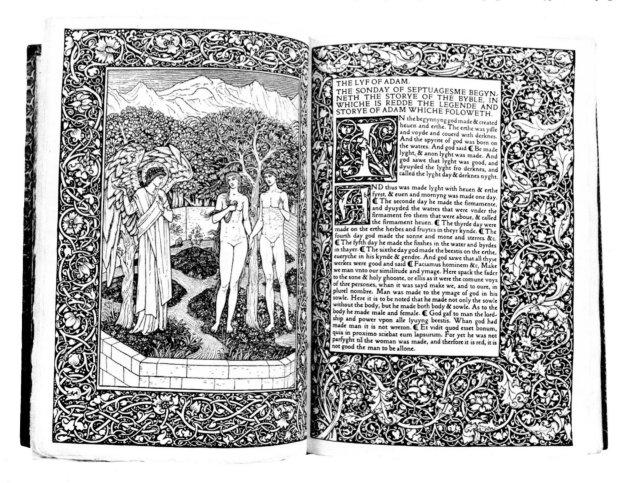

Ornate scrollwork sets off both text and picture in the 1892 edition of the Golden Legend—selections from the Bible. The book was pub- lished by the Kelmscott Press, founded in London by the poet William Morris. It was the first modern press to emphasize fine printing.

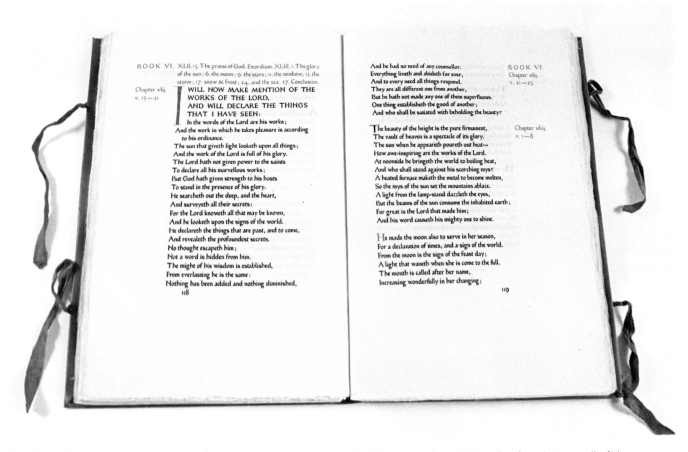

This fine Ashendene Press volume reproduces a single book of the Bible, Ecclesiasticus. The ribbons on the front and back can be tied to hold the covers closed. Prices of such "private-press" editions vary; an Ashendene printing of Ecclesiasticus sold in 1971 for $1,000.

MUSEUMS AND LIBRARIES
American Bible Society
New York, New York 10023

Bridwell Library, Southern Methodist University
Dallas, Texas 75275

Henry E. Huntington Library
San Marino, California 91108

The New York Public Library
New York, New York 10018

Northern Bible Society Bible Museum
Duluth, Minnesota 55802

The Pierpont Morgan Library
New York, New York 10016

COLLECTORS ORGANIZATIONS
International Bible Collectors Society
P.O. Box 2485
El Cajon, California 92021

BOOKS
The Cambridge History of the Bible, 3 vols., Cambridge University Press, 1963-1970.

Herbert, A. S., ed., *Historical Catalogue of Printed Editions of the English Bible 1525-1961.* Revised edition of T. H. Darlow and H. F. Moule, 1903. American Bible Society, 1968.

Hills, Margaret T., ed., *The English Bible in America: A Bibliography of Editions of the Bible and the New Testament Published in America 1777-1957.* American Bible Society and The New York Public Library, 1961.

Rumball-Petre, Edwin A. R., *Rare Bibles.* Philip C. Duschnes, 1954. (Second edition, revised)

Simms, P. Marion, *The Bible in America.* Wilson-Erickson, 1936.

Wright, John, *Early Bibles of America.* T. Whittaker, 1894.

Bicycles
From Boneshaker to Safety

I must have sounded pretty convincing one day a few years ago, when I ran down an airport corridor shouting, "I have to get on that plane!" The 727 was already taxiing toward the runway, but the gate attendant called it back on his walkie-talkie and I scrambled aboard gratefully. I did not explain to the other passengers, for only a fellow collector would have understood the urgency of my mission. I had just learned that a bicycle was available in Sarasota.

It was a very special bicycle, an unusually rare four-wheeled model, or quadricycle, made in 1850. I had

A lifelong fascination with machinery led David Metz, a businessman who lives in Freehold, New Jersey, to begin collecting old bicycles 20 years ago. He has avidly hunted, restored and ridden them ever since.

dreamed of owning it for four years, since first spotting it at a museum called Bellm's Cars and Music of Yesterday, whose owner finally became willing to sell the quadricycle. I have never told anyone how much I paid for it. When you find something you want that badly, price is not an insuperable obstacle. I was well rewarded for the frantic dash and expense. In 1976 at the convention of the Wheelmen, a nationwide collectors organization, my quadricycle won three major prizes.

I have another four-wheeler that took a lot of persistence to acquire. In 1970 I saw an advertisement for an auction in Pittsburgh. The sellers were three brothers, all in their seventies, who had been collecting old bicycles and other antiques all their lives. Disheartened by a spate of robberies, they had decided to sell out, and they were holding auctions every weekend. I attended one auction and bought three bikes.

Afterward, one of the brothers told me there was a quadricycle in one of the barns. I was ready to buy it on the spot, but he demurred since it was already consigned to the auctioneer and, besides, was hidden among so many other items that there was no way to get near it until that barn was emptied for sale.

High-wheelers, which were enormously popular during the 1880s and 1890s, line a wall of the author's garage. On the shelf are accessories of the same vintage: kerosene lamps, oilcans and tool bags.

So all I could do was wait. I phoned those brothers every weekend to keep tabs on the bike, and when it finally went on the block the following summer, I was there to bid. There were eight or 10 familiar faces taking part—as soon as I get to an auction, I can look around and tell who is interested in the bicycles—but none of them wanted that quadricycle as much as I did. It was such a rare one that instead of restoring it myself, as I would have with a lesser specimen, I gave it to a professional. It took him four years to complete the job.

On another occasion, I learned that a modern bicycle shop in Scarsdale, New York, had a bike made in the late 1870s. On my first visit, I rather diffidently offered to take it off the owner's hands. He said, "Oh, no, I'd never part with it." He said just about the same thing each time I came in—every three months for the next four years. But on my last visit, I noticed the bike was missing. The owner had moved it to a warehouse because he needed space in the shop. "Look," I said, "it shouldn't be hidden away like that. I'll put it on display. It will be preserved for years to come. What do you say?" He gave in.

The moral is that to be a collector of old cycles, you must be persistent and patient. I have been patient, and my collection runs to about 100 items now. I started with high-wheelers, also called ordinaries because they were the common bicycle in the late 19th Century. Many were made then, and they are fairly easy to find.

The oldest vehicle I own was made in 1850, but by that time the bicycle was hardly an exotic sight in Europe and America. It probably had been invented, in its most primitive form, several decades earlier.

There are, of course, students of the subject who are convinced that ancient cultures like the Egyptian and Sumerian possessed self-propulsion devices crudely similar to the bicycle. Others claim to see traces of such vehicles in frescoes excavated in Pompeii. In the church of Stoke Poges, Buckinghamshire, England, there is a stained-glass window—probably French or German in origin and dated 1642—in which a cherub sits on a two-wheeled vehicle that resembles a primitive bike. The trumpet that the cherub is blowing is regarded by some viewers as obviously a means of warning pedestrians.

Most authorities dismiss such claims, and virtually

When this Sawyer quadricycle was built in 1850, pedal-operated cycles were still experimental. The Sawyer's pedals activate a driving mechanism on the rear axle. Steering is done with a tiller fastened to both ends of the front axle. The Sawyer is entirely handmade.

every book on cycle history cites as the original bicycle the *célerifère,* which is said to have been demonstrated in Paris in 1791 by its inventor, a Comte de Sivrac. The fact is that this story is untrue. The *célerifère* was no bicycle but a horse-drawn carriage, imported into France in 1817 by Jean-Henry Sievrac. This mistake was discovered by Richard Walter Jeanes, professor of French at the University of Toronto, and was mentioned in Jeanes's Ph.D. dissertation when he was studying at the University of Paris in 1950. But his research went unnoticed until rediscovered recently by Jacques Seray. Accidentally or deliberately, French historians had twisted facts about de Sivrac, and in the process added a year to the fictitious *célerifère*'s invention date, 1791.

One factor in the misrepresentation was possibly French chauvinism. The bicycle historians picked up—and embroidered—the *célerifère* story from a book written by a French cyclist in 1891, not long after the bitter Franco-Prussian War. Given the circumstances, it was understandably difficult to give credit for the invention

where it was due, to a German, Baron Karl von Drais de Sauerbrun, who in 1818 patented his Draisienne, a wheeled hobbyhorse. Adult townspeople resented the commotion von Drais caused in the streets of Karlsruhe whenever he glided along on his contraption, but children delighted in the spectacle. Over the decades, von Drais, and then his memory, grew more and more beloved—in Karlsruhe, at least—and in 1891 a monument was erected to him there. Eventually the city named a school for von Drais and adorned it with a bas-relief of the Baron and his Draisienne.

The Draisienne represented the most elementary step toward fulfilling an age-old need: enabling people to move—under their own power—faster than when walking but with less effort. The prototype bicycle had a simple wood frame on carriage wheels and was operated like a child's scooter. It had no pedals. Except when coasting downhill, the seated rider propelled the bike by walking it with his feet on the ground. The only way to go uphill was to get off and push. The Draisienne's

This vélocipède, an early pedal-operated bicycle, has round wooden pedals rigidly attached to the hub of the front wheel. Since the only way to increase speed with this direct pedal drive was by enlarging the driving wheel, vélocipèdes evolved into high-wheelers.

impracticality, its substantial weight and uncomfortable ride, and the barrage of ridicule aimed at riders by scornful bystanders combined to keep the vehicle from achieving widespread popularity.

By 1839, however, Kirkpatrick Macmillan had improved the Draisienne by adding swinging pedals, which had to be pushed back and forth like pistons. About 20 years later, bicycle makers discovered they could make pedals more efficient by fastening them with cranks to the front wheel so that they could be pumped around by a circular motion of the feet. This increased speed and led to the additions of shoe-type brakes, precursor to handlebar-operated ones. The early rotary-pedal bicycle was known to the French as the *vélocipède*, a name whose derivation stresses speed. *Vélocipèdes* had forged iron frames, carpet-cloth padded seats and thin iron tires. The English, noting the effects of riding *vélocipèdes* over unpaved roads, nicknamed them "boneshakers."

Despite their jarring ride, boneshakers caught on quickly. Charles Dickens and other celebrities rode them. Racing was organized in Paris in 1868. The following year, the first bicycle journal—*Le Vélocipède Illustré*—was published, the first bicycle club was formed and the first bicycle exhibition was held in Paris. In the United States, a drawing in *Harper's Weekly* showed the new year, 1869, riding in on a boneshaker.

The Franco-Prussian War prevented the French bicycle industry from making progress in 1870 and 1871, and during those years, bicycle riding unaccountably passed out of vogue in the United States. But in England, the demand for bikes—preferably faster ones—continued to grow. Manufacturers began to enlarge the boneshaker's front wheel to increase the distance gained by each revolution of the pedals and thus increase speed. To offset the weight added to the front wheel, the back wheel was made smaller. This was the origin of the vehicle variously called the high-wheeler, the ordinary, or, more quaintly, the "penny-farthing"—an analogy between the wheels' size disparity and that of the largest and smallest of British coins. According to the

A high-wheeler, modified for stunt riding over Niagara Falls in the 1880s, has built-up rims that fit around a cable. The front wheel can be locked into position. The bicycle was balanced by the weight of the acrobat, who sat on a seat hung below the cable from arms attached to the front hub.

The 1887 Otto is 60 pounds of solid iron, but in its day it was regarded as a child's bike because of its simplicity.

Although the superiority of rotary pedals had long since been demonstrated, this 1885 Springfield had pedals that moved up and down.

This "spoon" brake, optional on the 1885 Star bicycle (left), presses the tire when activated by a lever on the handlebars.

The Star was designed to take the terror out of riding a high-wheeler. Placing the big driving wheel in the rear reduced the danger of a head-first plunge over the handlebars. But, since the imbalance had merely been reversed, the Star introduced the risk of a backward fall.

Driving action of the Star's pedals reached the rear wheel through gear mechanisms inside drums attached to the rear hub.

1978 edition of the *Guinness Book of World Records*, the front wheel of the world's largest high-wheeler, owned by Paul Niquette of New Canaan, Connecticut, is 64 inches in diameter. It cost Niquette about $3,500 to buy the bike and have it restored.

The high-wheelers became enormously popular—by 1878, there were 50,000 of them in England—but their heyday was short because they were so dangerous. Since the rider was perched over the front axle, as much as 5 feet off the ground, a pothole or bump in the road could send him flying over the handlebars in a header. "Falling forwards from a bicycle is by no means a difficult exploit," wrote Viscount Bury in an 1887 volume on the sport. "Indeed, the difficulty is to avoid performing it." When the bike was tearing downhill, the brakes were incapable of stopping it. Since the pedals turned with every revolution of the front wheel, riders often coasted with their legs sticking out to the sides. In a header, legs and handlebars often tangled, aggravating the disaster. Prudent cyclists sped downhill with their legs draped over the handlebars. That way, they could be thrown clear of the vehicle and, with luck, land on a hedge or some other relatively soft feature of the landscape.

To reduce the dangers, some manufacturers reversed the configuration, putting the large wheel in back and the small one in front. I own a bike of this sort, a Star, which I found by accident. I had stopped at a gas station in Pennsylvania, on my way home from an auction in New England, with a high-wheeler hanging out of my trunk. The attendant said he had seen one like it chained to a fence outside an antique store. His directions were vague and it was already dark, but I followed the lead and found the bike: a high-wheeler, all right, but with the high wheel in back. It took me six months to persuade the owner to sell it to me at a reasonable price.

All sorts of tricycles and quadricycles were also invented to spare riders the hazards of mounting a high-wheeler. Such cycles are difficult for American collectors to find because they did not enjoy the commercial success in the United States that they experienced in

Getting On and Off a High-Wheeler

The author, wearing his cycle-club uniform, begins to mount by pushing the bicycle ahead while holding it upright. He straddles the rear wheel and puts his left foot on the mounting step above it.

As momentum from the push keeps the high-wheeler moving ahead, the rider thrusts his right foot forward to the pedal. As the pedal is moved around by the turning wheel, it pulls him toward the seat.

England. These multiwheelers are the prizes of every collection that includes them. Eventually, chain drive was introduced in these cycles, and it revolutionized the industry. The chain sprockets could be of unequal size to provide the gearing advantage previously attained by using a dangerously large driving wheel; and thus came the modern bicycle—known originally as the safety—with wheels of equal size.

Champions of the high-wheeler scorned the safety bicycle as a "dwarf" and claimed it had one inherent danger of its own. But *Wheeling,* a British journal of the 1880s, refuted the argument of the high-wheeler faction by asserting: "The old objection that you are down

where the dogs can reach you is balanced by the fact that you can more easily kick the canine."

Dogs or no dogs, the safety's nearly universal acceptance doomed the high-wheeler. By 1893, it was no longer manufactured, and the safety bicycle, ruler of the road, was being improved in a number of ways: lightweight materials were used, improved gearing systems were developed and rubber tires were perfected.

Since all the important developments took place before 1900, I collect only bicycles made before that date. Still, safeties made during the first part of the 20th Century offer relatively inexpensive investments for a beginning collector because they are considerably easier

The quickest way to dismount—known to enthusiasts as the emergency dismount—is to take both feet off the pedals at once and jump backward over the rear wheel, landing on both feet simultaneously.

A more cautious method of dismounting is the reverse of mounting. The rider moves his left foot from the pedal to the mounting step. Then he swings his right foot down to the ground.

to find. Early safeties still turn up occasionally at flea markets and auctions, but older bikes almost never do. Sometimes it is possible to buy an antique bike from a collector with duplicates, and museums are sometimes willing to buy or trade old cycles, especially automobile museums that include cycles as the forerunners of cars.

Another good way to find old bicycles is through membership in the Wheelmen, an organization to which most serious collectors belong. It has more than 500 members, and chapters in 13 states. Wheelmen is modeled on the first American bicycle clubs, formed in the 1880s for protection against teamsters, who often reacted violently when cyclists scared their horses. The clubs

were based in cities—few countryfolk of the period took to cycling—and were made up of well-educated, affluent adventure seekers. Each club had its own uniform, the components of which—caps, shirts, trousers—are now considered eminently collectible. Many of the clubs united in 1881 to form the League of American Wheelmen, whose purpose was to lobby for better roads and for the rights of cyclists. The League, which had 120,000 members by 1884, made the first measurements of distances between many cities and posted some of the first danger and stop signs.

Like clubs of the 1880s, chapters of modern Wheelmen have banners and uniforms—members of my chap-

An 1885 Columbia, called a "two-track" because the third wheel is directly in front of the right rear wheel, is one of many tricycles designed during the 1870s and 1880s to make cycling safer. How- ever, because the rider sat directly above the axle, the Columbia could tip backward when going up a steep hill. To prevent it from going all the way over, an anti-tip pole was fastened to the rear of the seat.

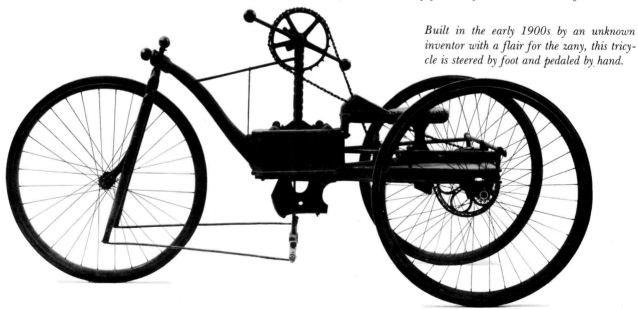

Built in the early 1900s by an unknown inventor with a flair for the zany, this tricycle is steered by foot and pedaled by hand.

Extraordinarily versatile, the Coventry Club-Tandem quadricycle, made in 1886, can be ridden by two persons or by one in either the front or back seat. With the rear wheel detached, it becomes a tricycle. A differential gear allows the wheels to turn at different speeds around corners. Original owners of these bikes sometimes put motors on the tricycle version, creating forerunners of the automobile.

ter wear navy-blue knee-length trousers, dark stockings, short-sleeved white shirts, gold-trimmed caps and red bow ties—and stage frequent riding exhibitions. New members have to ride a high-wheeler for at least 10 miles. The Wheelmen put out a semiannual magazine and a quarterly newsletter full of advice on how to learn to ride a high-wheeler, make a leather saddle and re-spoke wheels or straighten them. The newsletter also offers information on shopping for antique bikes.

The value of an old bike depends largely on how many of its parts are original. If a bike is in fairly good condition, it is often best to leave it alone, rather than restore it. To restore a bike, you often have to have replacement parts specially made, although original parts can be found. I was lucky enough once to buy a lot of parts from a bicycle shop in Brooklyn that was closing. The owner had been in that store for 50 years, and the shop had been there awhile before he came.

A collector with a sharp eye can spot a beat-up bike that can be restored easily. Once, when I was browsing in an antique shop in New Hope, Pennsylvania, I saw a very early safety bike hanging up near the rafters. It looked rather dilapidated—its worn seat was hanging loose. But I saw that it had all the main parts. I bought the bike for $10, took it home and restored it, and it turned out to be a beautiful safety worth about $350.

It might take a beginner a while to be able to match that coup, but anyone can put my most important collecting technique into practice right away: Do not take no for an answer. Time after time, tenacity has paid off. There are only a few more bikes that I need for my collection. I know a fellow who has one, and I've been after him for quite a while. Last time I spoke to him, he said he still wasn't quite ready to break down, but he promised me that I would be the first person he would call in case he changed his mind. I'll get that bike yet.

Modern, chain-driven two-wheelers of this sort were called safety bicycles: they were less likely to tip, easier to balance and, if balance was lost, dropped the rider for a lesser fall. This deluxe Columbia Light Roadster came with a kerosene lamp, chain guard and spring-mounted seat.

The Roadster's front-wheel fork has springs to smooth the ride. The spokes cross for extra strength and rigidity.

Billing his invention as "a thing of such unique construction that to be admired needs but introduction," Sterling Elliott of Massachusetts offered the public the Elliott Hickory Safety Bicycle in 1888. He had a mystical belief in the moral superiority of wood. He declared, "It has been our aim to build a bicycle that a man or woman could ride, and still be a Christian."

As the front fork shows, the hickory bicycle Elliott made for men does not have the spoon brake typical of the age. He provided spoon brakes on the crossbar-less women's model.

Chivalry inspired the design of this tandem, built in the late 1890s and intended for couples. Unlike most two-seaters, it cannot be steered from the front seat, which was meant to be occupied by the woman.

There are stationary armrests instead of handlebars, and footrests on the front fork. Thus, the gentleman in the rear seat, who had to do all the steering, might have ended up doing all the pedaling, too.

EVOLUTION OF THE BICYCLE

1818 : the Draisienne, a steerable, foot-propelled wooden horse with medium-sized wheels—like an overgrown scooter—built by Baron Karl von Drais de Sauerbrun in Germany

1839 : the first pedal-driven cycle, a two-wheeler built by Kirkpatrick Macmillan in Scotland

1861 : the *vélocipède*, or boneshaker, driven with pedals attached to an enlarged front wheel, introduced first in France and then England

1870 : the Ariel, an all-metal high-wheeler with gears that converted one revolution of the pedals into two of the front wheel, built by James K. Starley and William Hillman in England

1871 : the Tension high-wheeler, with spokes that could be adjusted individually, built by W. H. J. Grout in England

1879 : the Bicyclette safety, with rear chain drive, built by H. J. Lawson in England

1885 : the diamond-framed Rover safety, prototype of today's standard bicycle, built in England by James K. Starley, coinventor of the Ariel *(above)*, and William Sutton

MUSEUMS
Henry Ford Museum
Dearborn, Michigan 48121

Indian Motorcycle Museum
Springfield, Massachusetts 01109

Museum of Science and Industry
Chicago, Illinois 60637

Smithsonian Institution
Washington, D.C. 20560

COLLECTORS ORGANIZATIONS
The Wheelmen, c/o Don Adams
Henry Ford Museum
Dearborn, Michigan 48121

BOOKS
Alderson, Frederick, *Bicycling: A History.* Praeger Publishers, 1972.

Caunter, C. F., *The History and Development of Cycles.* Her Majesty's Stationery Office, 1950.

Palmer, Arthur Jackson, *Riding High: The Story of the Bicycle.* E. P. Dutton and Company, Inc., 1956.

Ritchie, A., *King of the Road.* Ten Speed Press, 1975.

Books
The Fascination of the Printed Page

A storage warehouse in New York City was throwing out some household goods that had been left unclaimed for many years. The owner of the warehouse told his employees to take anything they were willing to carry off; the rest would go into the garbage.

One of the movers poked through the heap and spotted an old book with exceedingly banged-up covers. It was printed in peculiar, old-looking type. The workman stuffed the book into his lunch bag, along with his

---

For six years, as head of the book department of the New York auction house Sotheby Parke Bernet, Jerry E. Patterson observed at close range the shifting patterns of book collecting.

---

chopped-egg sandwich, because he happened to be delivering some things to an auction gallery later that day and decided he would ask the auctioneer if the book might be of any value.

The auctioneer saw at a glance that the volume was a rare 16th Century English book, John Lyly's *Euphues, or the Anatomy of Wit*, published in 1578 and a landmark in early English literature. It was soon sold at auction for $8,500. This substantial sum, minus the auction gallery's commission, went to the mover—a nice reward for his curiosity and luck.

In another city at another time, a dealer in rare books looked over stacks waiting to be auctioned and came across a volume of poetry by Edna St. Vincent Millay. It was a title that was ordinarily worth about $10. However, this copy had been signed in front with the name Nancy Boyd. The bookdealer recalled that Nancy Boyd was a pseudonym that had been used by Millay before she became well known. Books signed by her with that name are now rare and quite valuable. That observant dealer was rewarded for his knowledge of literary history with a choice bargain.

Not everyone who rummages in old books will have

The middle shelf (opposite) holds original editions of works by Mark Twain, all clean, complete copies in their original bindings. Many collectors begin by assembling the works of a favorite author.

the moving man's luck or the dealer's expertise. But anyone who takes up book collecting will experience the excitement of discovering books he has been searching for: the fine first edition that fills out a shelf of other choice volumes, the tattered treatise that only a few other collectors have been able to unearth. With diligence reinforced by knowledge, the booklover can assemble a collection that not only will give him a sense of personal satisfaction, but also will have historical significance. He may also discover that as his collection expands and gathers hard-to-find items it increases remarkably in monetary value.

The knowledge needed to make a start in book collecting is not very extensive. A few book collectors' terms have to be learned. Then it is primarily a matter of choosing which corner of the immense world of books to concentrate on.

Few book collectors set out to assemble shelves of every sort of book. The field is far too broad: some 150 million different works have been published since Johann Gutenberg produced the first printed book about 1455. As a result, nearly all book collectors specialize. Some restrict their collecting to detective fiction, or Bibles, or children's books or even cookbooks—fields so unusual that they are discussed in separate articles in this encyclopedia.

Other collectors specialize in one of the six areas discussed on the following pages. These subdivisions of the broad avocation are the most popular today: sports books *(pages 104-105);* medical and scientific books *(page 107);* the works of great or "classic" authors *(pages 108-111);* Americana, the term denoting early or rare books about America *(pages 101-103);* the especially handsome limited editions produced by small publishers and called press books *(pages 112-113);* and first editions of modern American authors *(pages 114-117).*

In all the diverse areas of book collecting, the most sought-after books are firsts: the first book written on a particular subject, the first book printed in a certain locality—but above all, first editions. The first edition of almost any book is bound to be more valuable than subsequent editions. Strictly for reading enjoyment, a later edition suffices, but for collecting, a first is best. In conversations among book collectors, that is the sentiment most often heard. One collector cannot mention the title of a book without another collector inquiring: "Is it a first?" A firm grasp of the meaning of edition is absolutely necessary for the serious book collector because, more often than not, the pricing of collectible books is based on the edition.

The term "first edition" needs explanation because its meaning has been altered as various economic and technological developments changed the way books are printed. Before 1800, printers generally broke up the carefully set page forms that a book was printed from immediately after they had run off the first printed version. They disassembled the forms and carefully distributed the type—one piece for each letter—into the compartments of their type drawers. Metal type was expensive, and typesetter's labor was cheap. If the book became popular and a second edition was called for, the typesetter had to pick the costly type back out of the drawers and reset the pages, piece by piece. The first and second editions of any book of that era were inevitably quite distinct.

Since 1800, however, publishers have increasingly asked the printers who work with them to leave the type intact in the page forms after printing a first run of, say, 5,000 copies. Then if considerable public demand for the book develops, the printer simply puts the same forms of previously set type back on the press and runs off a second "impression." Strictly speaking, both the first and second pressruns or impressions are first editions; the type has not changed.

But both pressruns are not truly firsts. One run precedes the other, and therefore only the first impression—the copies that are run off the first time the press prints the work—has additional value. In modern usage first impressions, and only these, are universally called first editions, and this is the term you will find in catalogues issued by bookdealers and in magazines that are devoted to book collecting.

Despite George Bernard Shaw's self-deprecating remark about his second editions being rarer than his first, for most authors the first edition of a work is the scarcest and the most collectible. In virtually every case the first is the edition closest to what the author originally wrote. The publishing histories of a number of classic works show that mistakes have gradually crept into most editions after the first. If the book has been illustrated, the pictures in the first edition are likely to appear clearer and sharper. This is especially true of books that were printed before the 20th Century.

To realize the importance of the first edition it is necessary to think of the book as a collectible object—an object of art, in fact. The first edition is an original to book collectors, and they would rather own it than a later printing, exactly as a collector of paintings prefers an original to a copy.

Fiction first editions tend to be more difficult to identify than nonfiction. That is because novels and poetry are generally printed in more editions than are nonfiction works. For any type of book, however, you can usually find clues to the edition. Nowadays many publishers helpfully include the words "first edition" or "second edition" on the page of the book that contains the copyright notice (in most American books, on the back of the title page). Other publishers do not do this but rather, if the book is not a first edition, may so inform the buyer by printing a notice near the copyright date that says something like, "Reprinted in 1975, 1977." Obviously, a reprint is not a first.

If there is no information at all concerning edition, the collector must find out in what year the book was originally published and compare this date with the publication date, which usually appears either with the copyright notice or on the title page, below the publisher's name. In older books the date may be found in the colophon, which is the printer's statement concerning the book's publication. The colophon appears at the end of the volume.

While the first edition of a modern book is defined as the first impression or pressrun—the first appearance of the book in print—there may be variations even within a first edition. Corrections can be, and frequently are, made during the initial pressrun. A printer may discover, when he examines the first few copies coming off the press, that a comma is missing on page 5, or that the page number has somehow been omitted at the bottom of page 106. He then stops the press, makes the correction and starts printing again. Subsequent copies that come off the press are therefore slightly different from the initial, uncorrected ones. Thus is born a second "state" or "issue."

An example of a first edition with issue differences is Pearl Buck's famous novel of China, *The Good Earth,* published in 1931. In the first few copies, in line 17 of page 100, "flees" was misprinted for "fleas." The misprint was caught and fixed. The copies containing the misprint are listed in booksellers' catalogues as "first edition, first issue," while subsequent corrected copies are "first edition, second issue." (Confusingly, some dealers refer to second issues as second impressions.) Almost always, the first, uncorrected issue is considered to be the more valuable: in book collecting the emphasis is placed on the earliest.

A change in binding can also result in a second issue. If halfway through the first pressrun the binder runs through one bolt of cloth for the book's covers and spine, and changes to another, he has created a second issue within the first edition, since the two bolts will probably vary slightly in color.

The little clues, such as misprints and altered bindings, that enable a booklover to identify which issue of a book he has in hand are called points. A famous point is the gross misprinting of an entire line in the first issue of *The Cloister and the Hearth,* an 1861 novel by British author Charles Reade. Before it was corrected, the line read: "She threw her head over her apron." A collector of 19th Century British novels who comes across that misprinted line in a copy knows he has the very first version of Reade's book.

An example of a point that is not a misprint is found in the first edition of Ernest Hemingway's *A Farewell to Arms,* which has two issues. The first issue does not contain the usual printed notice stating, "None of the characters in this book is a living person." This disclaimer was inserted in the second issue to forestall protests by certain of Hemingway's friends who thought—with good reason—that they were the originals of the characters in the novel.

Another famous point is in the dedication of General Lew Wallace's Biblical classic *Ben Hur.* The first printings had a dedication page that read: "To the Wife of My Youth," suggesting that she might already be dead. General Wallace was said to have been the recipient of some interesting letters from single ladies. Mrs. Wallace, who was very much alive, insisted that the dedication in later editions be changed to read: "To the Wife of My Youth Who Still Abides with Me."

Knowing what the first edition is, and how to recognize it, is not of course the same as finding it. Some first editions cannot be procured at any price. Only a single copy has ever been found of the little book containing the letter that Christopher Columbus wrote to the treasurer of King Ferdinand and Queen Isabella telling of his discovery of a new world. Printed in Barcelona in March 1493, this diminutive book of only four leaves is considered by most experts to be the single greatest piece of Americana. Since 1892 this rarity, beside which the Gutenberg Bible is positively common, has been kept in The New York Public Library. The Columbus letter has been appropriately called "the black swan in the book collector's pond." But sought-after first editions are not necessarily ancient. Of Robert Frost's first book of poems, *Twilight,* printed in 1894, only two copies are known to exist.

The best way to learn about firsts, issues and points is to study the invaluable aids called bibliographies. A bibliography gives the printing history of the works of one author, or of all of the works on one subject. Few areas of collectible books lack standard bibliographies. While they vary widely in accuracy and comprehensiveness, they all list first editions and tell the collector how to distinguish them. The bibliographies also tell what a complete copy should include—the number of illustrative plates, for example.

Bibliographies are so vital a part of book collecting that booksellers' catalogues customarily cite a bibliographical reference after each catalogue entry. This enables collectors to know exactly what book is being advertised. Collectors of Americana soon become familiar with the word "Sabin," followed by a number, in booksellers' catalogues. The reference is to the *Dictionary of Books Relating to America from its Discovery to the Present Time,* edited in 29 volumes by Joseph Sabin and a host of succeeding editors between 1868 and 1939. Catalogues listing modern American literature cite Merle Johnson's *American First Editions*.

Beginning collectors can discover what bibliographies exist on an author or subject by visiting a local library. Library catalogues have a section under each subject in which bibliographies are listed along with other reference works, and reference librarians are familiar with bibliographies of all kinds—including the *World Bibliography of Bibliographies*.

The appropriate bibliographies should be the first purchase of a collector as soon as he has settled on the area in which he will specialize. Since bibliographies are usually rather cumbersome volumes poorly suited to being carried in a pocket, the next step is to make a convenient checklist of the first editions you are most interested in—including their dates of publication and other pertinent data.

Bibliographies come in handy in a number of ways that become apparent only after you have studied one. Even a quick study of an author's bibliography may reveal unsuspected facts about his work, and alert the collector to watch for special items. The first book published by American novelist Sinclair Lewis, for example, was written under the pseudonym Tom Graham in 1912; it was a boy's book, *Hike and the Aeroplane*. The first book of another famous novelist, Edith Wharton, was a volume of poetry; her second, a work of nonfiction on interior decoration. The truly fervent collector of first editions of Sinclair Lewis' work, or Edith Wharton's, will want to look for these volumes despite the fact that they are not the kinds of works for which the author became well known.

The next step is to locate specialist dealers. A good way to do this is to consult the *AB Bookman's Weekly* or *The Book Collector*. Both are magazines carrying the advertisements of hundreds of specialist bookdealers in the United States and abroad. Most dealers will mail you their current catalogue free—and continue to send subsequent catalogues as long as you occasionally buy something from them. And the catalogues themselves are useful guides to prices and desirability of editions similar to the ones listed.

Many books are prized for reasons that have nothing to do with a particular edition. If the volume has been signed by the author, it possesses additional value for the collector. When the writer has signed his name and also the name of the person to whom he gave the book, the volume is known as a presentation copy. If the inscription in the book is to the writer's wife, mistress or sweetheart—or even to a parent or a close friend—the volume has greater value than one that was inscribed to an unknown admirer. And if the author has employed a seldom-used pseudonym, the value of the copy skyrock-

Books flow from a cornucopia in a bookplate created by Valentin Le Campion around 1945 for an American collector.

Angels pray in a delicate 19th Century-style bookplate drawn by the British book illustrator Robert Anning Bell.

Collectible Bookplates

Collectors of bookplates, which are the pasted-on labels used since the mid-15th Century to indicate ownership of books, often do more than collect—they employ artists to design bookplates for them, and then trade these with other collectors for *their* private plates. A single collector may commission dozens of plates during a lifetime, employing top-flight artists to design them, such as the noted illustrator Rockwell Kent.

This practice of exchanging unique personal bookplates with other collectors adds extra spice to the pursuit of old and rare bookplates, and plates designed by famous artists or owned by famous men. Bookplates have identified the books of notable men as varied as Samuel Pepys and George Washington. Great artists who have done bookplates include Dürer, Holbein, Hogarth, Manet and Toulouse-Lautrec. A famous statesman and artist who designed his own bookplate was patriot-silversmith Paul Revere.

Bookplates have gone through many fashions. Early ones reproduced owners' coats of arms *(right, middle)*. Romantic landscapes became popular in the 19th Century. Increasingly, 20th Century bookplates have borne austere designs, many suggesting the collector's profession *(below)*.

Bookplates may be attached to books or loose. If a book is valuable because of its former owner, his bookplate should stay in it. To remove an interesting bookplate from an otherwise ordinary volume, use a soft watercolor brush and warm water to wet the plate thoroughly, and a razor blade or craftsman's knife to lift the plate free. Use blotting paper to dry the plate.

Most collectors keep their loose bookplates in envelopes or boxes, or lightly hinged to mounts. Pasting plates into albums makes their removal or rearrangement inconvenient.

The best way for a would-be collector to start is to contact The American Society of Bookplate Collectors and Designers at 429 North Stoneman Avenue, Alhambra, California 91801. The Society can put you in touch with the nearest bookplate club.

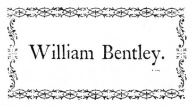

The bookplate of a Salem, Massachusetts, clergyman who died in 1819 is as plain as an unadorned Puritan church.

The device of Britain's Order of the Garter identifies this plate as Lord Rosebery's, although his name is absent.

A woman's face peers from a rib cage in a bizarre plate designed for a Dutch doctor.

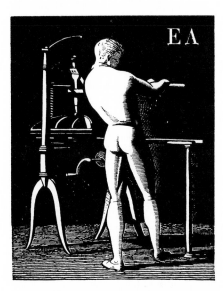

"EA" is Elmer Adler, a New York printer whose plate was designed by Rockwell Kent.

A locomotive chugs past the pagan deity Fauna in a railroadman's bookplate.

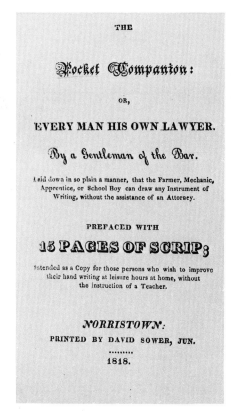

Fine plates of a raccoon and a skunk, native animals that fascinated early European travelers to America, decorate a 1770 book.

Books published by Benjamin Franklin, the most notable printer of colonial America, are highly valued by Americana collectors.

An early imprint from a small, local printer in Norristown, Pennsylvania, is a legal "how-to" book published in 1818.

A stark engraving of the Statehouse in Philadelphia embellishes a book by Englishman Henry Wansey about his travels to America in 1796.

ets, as the dealer who spotted Millay poems inscribed "Nancy Boyd" was well aware.

Collectors learn which writers are likely to have autographed presentation copies of their books and which are not. Charles Dickens did not like signing his books, even for friends, and usually refused requests to do so. Inscribed copies of Dickens' works are therefore rare and expensive. Other writers, such as Henry Wadsworth Longfellow, complained about signing, but nevertheless signed, and presentation copies are not difficult to find. In the case of still others, such as Edwin Arlington Robinson, it is said that unsigned copies of their works are rarer than the signed ones. Although Robinson was twice the winner of the Pulitzer Prize, his volumes of poetry were usually saved only by the friends and acquaintances to whom he sent signed copies.

Book collectors also ascribe extra value to volumes that have been owned by famous people. A book that once was owned by George Washington, although remarkable in no other way, will have value. You can deduce previous ownership, called provenance, from several clues. In previous centuries important men often had their library books rebound in fine leather that was stamped with their initials or coat of arms. Less costly and therefore more popular identifications were bookplates *(pages 96-97)*—printed or engraved labels pasted into books to show ownership. Other men simply signed their names inside their library volumes. Books that are thus associated with well-known people are called, logically enough, association copies.

While many of the factors affecting the value of a book, like signatures and dates, are readily identified, others are not. For one thing, there are shifting fashions in book collecting. The editions that are most sought after change not only from generation to generation, but even from decade to decade. Literary reputations rise and fall over the years, and the collectible-book market rises and falls accordingly.

Consider the case of the English novelist John Galsworthy, who wrote in the first decades of this century. In the 1920s Galsworthy was a favorite with collectors, who paid hundreds of dollars for first editions of his books. But Galsworthy's literary reputation faded, and the prices of his first editions fell in response. Then in the early 1970s, doubtless because of the popularity of television programs based on Galsworthy's *Forsyte Saga,* his reputation began to rise, and interest in collecting first editions of his work revived.

A number of authors are always collected, untouched by changing literary fashions—Shakespeare, Dr. Samuel Johnson, Byron, Shelley, Jane Austen and a number of other writers of the first rank. The collector of such classic authors soon discovers that the prices charged for their works remain consistently high. Only a collector of

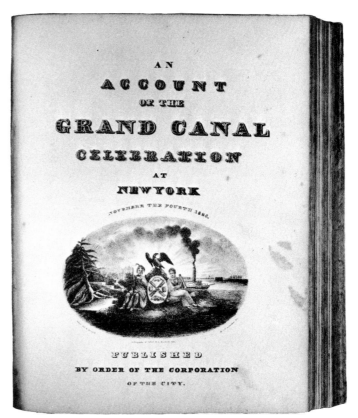

This book commemorates the 1825 opening of the Erie Canal, which connected the Great Lakes and the Atlantic. The completion of the canal was an important milestone in young America's progress.

A view of Niagara Falls illustrates John Hinton's "History and Topography of the U.S.," published in London in the 1830s. Many European books showed America's wonders in hand-colored plates.

considerable resources can hope ever to locate and acquire a complete set of the first editions of, say, the poetry of Lord Byron.

If the author is the focus of a collection, works later than the first editions may be desirable. Some collectors specialize in later editions of their favorite author's work when there is something notable about them—a new introduction, perhaps, or excellent illustrations. Other collectors look for adaptations of the author's work for the stage, and translations. Later-than-firsts, adaptations and translations are cheaper than first editions and hence good areas for the beginner.

Even a rather rare and valuable item loses much worth if the copy is a mess. A book should be in what the catalogues call fine condition—clean and free of stains. The pages should not be dog-eared, and there should be no scribbling or underlining in the text. The covers must be clean, and they should not show wear around the edges. The corners should not be bent or "bumped," as the bookseller's description terms it. Prospective buyers should remember to look carefully at the top and bottom of the book's spine, because wear is likely to appear there first. The value of old leatherbound books will increase if the leather is in good condition, and especially if it is "morocco," a fine tanned goatskin originally developed in North Africa but produced since in several countries.

The emphasis on collecting only books in good physical condition is relatively new. In the past, collectors were rather lackadaisical even about ascertaining whether a book was complete. Today any book, even a relatively rare edition, is assigned a high value only if all pages are present—the original blank leaves at the beginning and end, the half title (the page before the title page that carries the title of the book in abbreviated form) and dedication page.

Books are often harmed by fire, but the most common enemy of books is water. Water-staining, damp-staining and "foxing" are serious hazards for the collector. Foxing is a moisture-related, light-brown spotting that eventually mars the pages of many older books. Caused by traces of iron or fungus in the paper, it is called foxing because the spots resemble the paw prints of the animal. Foxing sharply reduces the value of a book, and a water-damaged or damp-stained volume is in most cases unsalable to a collector.

Whoever the author or whatever the subject collected, it is always wise to try for the best available copy of any book. Sometimes it is necessary to settle for slightly less than the best, with the aim of upgrading as soon as possible by buying a better copy and disposing of the inferior one. Good copies are those that increase most in value. An old maxim among experienced book people runs, "Good copies get better but poor copies don't."

While condition, provenance and edition have a profound effect on the desirability of a book, one additional factor is much less important than is commonly supposed. That is age. Although many first editions are indeed old, age in itself does not necessarily make a book more valuable. A battered tome found among some old, long-neglected family possessions may turn out to have great value, like the copy of Lyly's *Euphues* discovered by the moving man. More likely, though, it will have little if any value.

The age of books brought for appraisal to booksellers and auction galleries almost always is stressed by prospective sellers. "I have an old book" is doubtless the preliminary remark heard most often in such places. The assumption that age enhances value is based partly on another assumption, which is that older books are hard to come by; often, such is not the case. Many more books have been printed in the past than most people suspect. During the first 50 years of printing, in the second half of the 15th Century, an estimated 40,000 different books, called incunabula, were printed. From that time until today, the printing presses have never fallen still. It is by no means difficult to purchase a 17th or 18th Century book; most booksellers in large cities will have at least a few examples on hand. Many of these books are priced at less than $50.

Many quite old books were written by authors who never achieved fame, or by authors who are long, and deservedly, forgotten. Modern books, especially if they are printed in small first editions, may be many times more valuable than older works that were published in large editions. Books written by notable authors before they achieved fame are likely to have been printed in small numbers and to have become scarce—and valuable. One such rarity is William Faulkner's first book, a slim volume of poems called *The Marble Faun*, first published in 1924. To take advantage of the potential of early works, a famous New York City bookseller used to encourage beginning collectors to regularly purchase the first book published by any promising author. The premise was simple but the judgment required to act upon it is not: promising writers do not always achieve a good reputation later in their careers.

But the best path to follow in book collecting is the one taken by thousands of predecessors—browsing in secondhand bookshops with a bibliography close at hand. While great rarities are not likely to be found, you will certainly run across many interesting items while you enjoy the search.

For related material, see the article on Bibles in this volume, and the articles on Children's Books, Cookbooks and Detective Fiction in separate volumes of The Encyclopedia of Collectibles.

Americana

Americana, a favorite field of collecting in the United States, consists of two kinds of books. One category represents early or unusual ventures in American publishing; the other, books about America, published either here or abroad.

The earliest examples of Americana are of course the books printed in Europe soon after 1492, describing the New World. These are very expensive—beyond the reach of the average person. So are the earliest books published in America. Printing began in the American colonies in 1640, with publication of the *Bay Psalm Book* in Cambridge, Massachusetts. The progress of printing, however, was slow.

By the 18th Century, as printing presses became fairly common along the Eastern Seaboard, many more books appeared. This was especially true as the break with England approached. The American Revolution gave collectors of Americana a huge body of literature to choose from. For example, a collection can be made of contemporary accounts of Revolutionary naval battles or of the fighting in one or another of the colonies. Other collectible Americana from this period are books on architecture and inventions, and numerous books of sermons. While prices are high for some of these early volumes, many can be purchased for less than $100.

In the 19th Century, Americana subdivides into a number of categories. One of the most accessible for beginning collectors is that of the first books to be printed in a particular city, state or town. In general, any book printed in the first 10 years of printing's existence in a place is worth collecting. But so are the first books printed in that place on an important subject, such as the first medical book, the first law book, the first regional or local history.

Another 19th Century category generally neglected, and therefore good for beginners, is Americana published between the American Revolution and the Civil War. This was the period of the War of 1812, of rising interest in women's rights and of concern over the role of the American Indian, and each of these subjects inspired a wide range of books. And though the Civil War is not neglected by collectors, it also is a promising category. Here the numbers are immense and individual books are still modestly priced. Impressive collections have been put together, from books costing no more than $50 apiece, on such subjects as regimental histories—North or South—or books printed in the Confederate States during the War.

An even larger group of 19th Century Americana is

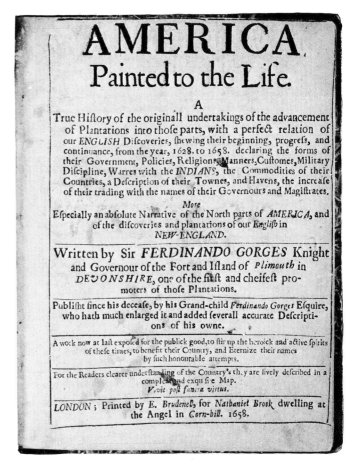

An old-fashioned title page from a book about what is now Maine is an example of Americana printed abroad—published in London in 1658 by the grandson of the author, Sir Ferdinando Gorges.

devoted to the history of U.S. expansion west of the Mississippi River. The core of such Western Americana is known as the Overland Narratives, the accounts published by people who crossed the plains and mountains on foot, by wagon or on horseback. The first Overland Narrative—and the foundation book of Western Americana—is the report written by Meriwether Lewis and William Clark of their exploration of the Louisiana Territory from 1804 to 1806 *(page 102)*.

But the single largest group of Overland Narratives probably is made up of the accounts written by travelers who participated in the famous California gold rush of 1849. Other areas of Western Americana from which a collection may be built include books about the settlement, exploration and development of each Western state; books about the Indian wars, the Mexican War and the cattle trade. The outlaws and badmen of the Old West are also the subject of many nonfiction books that are favorites with collectors. One bibliography in the field, Ramon Adams' *Six-Guns and Saddle Leather*, lists more than 2,000 books on Western outlaws.

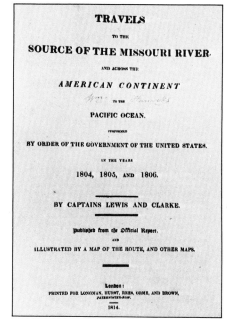

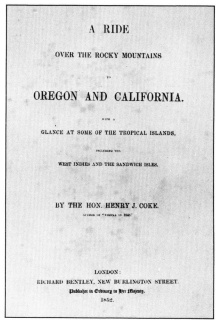

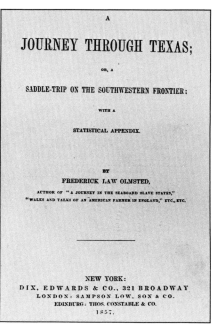

Misspelling and all (Clarke for Clark), Lewis and Clark's account of their explorations is precious Western Americana.

The title page of a book written by a young Englishman hides the drama of his Western trip, on which two people died.

Rare Western Americana is an account of early Texas by Frederick Law Olmsted, who later designed New York's Central Park.

An enraged buffalo puts a hunter to flight in an illustration by George Catlin, perhaps the greatest artist to record the early American West.

A Catlin plate records the look and dress of Plains Indians. Catlin volumes with the plates hand colored are prizes of Western Americana.

Sports

Fox hunting is a perennial favorite subject for sports-book collectors. A clean first edition of the 1928 classic above has brought $200.

Virtually every athletic diversion has been the subject of countless books, but the earliest writing on such pastimes in England and the United States was devoted almost exclusively to the sports of hunting and fishing. The oldest American sports book is Charles Bell's *Sportsman's Companion, or an Essay on Shooting,* which was published in New York in 1783. About four and a half centuries earlier, King Edward II's huntsman, Master William Twici, launched English sports literature with his *Le Art de Venery (The Art of Hunting),* written in Norman French.

The next major English sports book, published in 1486, is *The Boke of St. Albans.* It was written by a mysterious woman named Dame Juliana Berners, believed to have been a nun. *The Boke of St. Albans* consists of lists of beasts, and treatises on hawking, hunting and heraldry. A decade after its publication, Berners produced her *Treatyse on Fysshynge with an Angle.*

Berners' volume was the last word on the subject until

Hounds engulf horse and rider in a color plate by Sir Alfred Munnings, who illustrated "Hounds and Hunting through the Ages" (top).

1653, when Izaak Walton published *The Compleat Angler,* which continues to be considered a classic. Copies of this book are worth several hundred dollars apiece, depending upon their condition. In modern times, a number of famous authors—among them Zane Grey and Ernest Hemingway—have added their contributions to the collectible literature of fishing.

But a book need not be ancient or written by a celebrity to become desirable. Some fishing books, like Vincent Marinaro's *Modern Dry-Fly Code,* become instant classics because their contents fascinate anglers. *Modern Dry-Fly Code,* published at $6.95 in 1951, was worth $75 or so some three decades later.

Many of the sports books published in limited editions from 1927 to 1941 by one particular press, the Derrydale Press of New York City, have become almost prohibitively expensive, thanks to the interest of sportsmen-collectors. One especially popular volume, Charles Phair's *Atlantic Salmon Fishing,* was published in 1937 in a deluxe edition of 200 copies that originally cost $250 apiece, a price that rose at auction to about $4,500. A standard edition of 950 copies of Phair's book increased in price from $25 to $200. But several other Derrydale volumes, among them *Riding and Schooling Horses,* were

Ducks skim marsh grass in a color plate from the cover of Peter Scott's "Wild Chorus," published in 1938 but already sought after.

WILD
CHORUS

WRITTEN AND ILLUSTRATED BY
PETER SCOTT

COUNTRY LIFE LIMITED LONDON
NEW YORK CHARLES SCRIBNER'S SONS

Birds take wing in the frontispiece of "Wild Chorus," which was published in a limited edition of 1,250 copies, 1,200 of them signed by Scott.

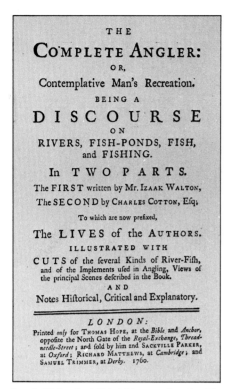

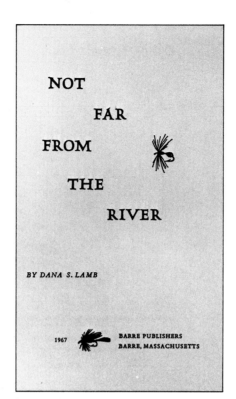

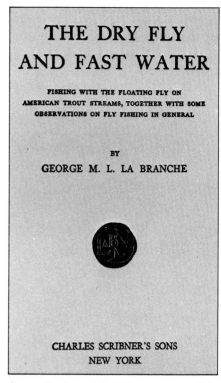

Izaak Walton's 1653 "Discourse"—the title page of the first edition is above—remains the most famous of books about fishing.

Some modern sports books, such as Dana S. Lamb's "Not Far from the River," quickly become sought-after classics of the type.

George La Branche's 1914 treatise on fishing discusses dry fly-fishing, but concentrates on casting for trout.

selling for less than $50 each during the late 1970s.

Many sports-book buffs look for fiction as eagerly as they do nonfiction. The libraries of such enthusiasts may contain first editions of the 19th Century English fox-hunting novels written by Robert Smith Surtees. Perhaps the all-time favorite of these is *Jorrocks's Jaunts and Jollities,* published in 1838. America's most famous sportsman-novelist may be Henry William Herbert, an expatriate Englishman who wrote historical novels and, beginning in the 1840s, published 10 books on sporting subjects under the name of Frank Forester. All of these books are widely collected, and beginners should be on the lookout for "Foresters" because their value is constantly increasing.

A few generations after Herbert's heyday, Burt Standish captivated young American readers with the fictional exploits of a multitalented college athlete named Frank Merriwell. Merriwell was such a popular hero that he appeared in about 245 books from 1896 to 1930. Copies of these books are fairly easy to locate and usually do not cost more than $10.

Baseball annuals, coveted by lovers of statistics, are also modestly priced. Sporting-goods firms churned them out in huge numbers during the early decades of the 20th Century. By 1975, copies of the *Spalding Guide Book* from the 1920s were selling for $15 to $20. Swap meets at which baseball cards are traded often are good places to find annuals and other baseball books.

Horse racing is nearly as notable as baseball for producing periodical volumes. Some collectors concentrate on finding annual studbooks. Others specialize in *The American Turf Register,* a periodical that began publication in 1829 and covered other sports as well as racing. Among its distinguished contributors was John James Audubon, the famous naturalist.

Knowledge of such details as Audubon's contributions is typical of the matters with which collectors concern themselves. They also make a point of identifying landmark books in individual fields of interest. They know, for example, that the first American book on archery is *The Archer's Manual, or the art of shooting with the long bow,* published anonymously in Philadelphia in 1830.

Experienced collectors also acquire a sense of the way in which regional differences affect the stocks of book-dealers. Copies of *The American Turf Register* are most plentiful in places where horse racing has been established since the 19th Century. Books on fox hunting are more likely to turn up at bookshops and book fairs in those parts of the country—Maryland and Virginia, for instance—where the sport is traditional. Books on boating and water sports are likely to be found on the seacoasts, and winter-sports books in New England.

Medicine and Science

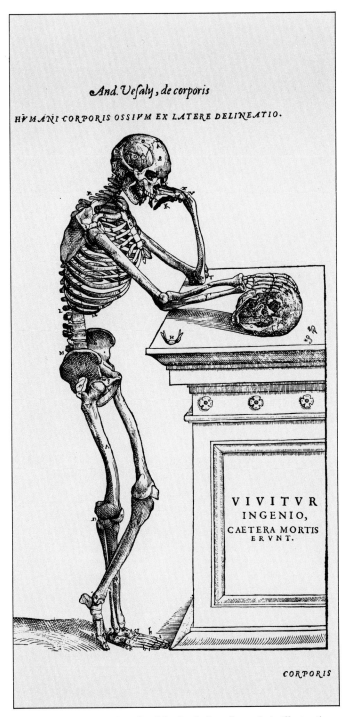

Part of the interest of medical books derives from their illustrations, many of which are of an artistic quality as high as that of this thoughtful skeleton in Vesalius' landmark 16th Century anatomy.

Many collectors of books on science or medicine specialize in first editions of works that changed medical or scientific history. Valuable medical books tend to be old, like James Parkinson's description of what became known as Parkinson's disease, *An Essay on the Shaking Palsey* (1817). In the physical sciences and mathematics, too, first editions of Sir Isaac Newton's *Quantitative Analyses Through Fluxions,* an explanation of calculus, and his *Opticks,* are treasures of museum caliber. But many important science books are modern. One is Robert Goddard's *A Method of Reaching Extreme Altitudes* (1919), describing principles used more than 50 years later to land on the moon. First editions of Einstein's works are also classics.

Copies of Goddard's book sold in the late 1970s for $500 to $750, and in 1975 a copy of the journal with Einstein's first piece on the theory of relativity sold for about $650. But many books of interest sell for reasonable prices. Some early editions of Sigmund Freud's works go for $25 to $50. Even lower prices are available in little-explored areas like biographies of famous doctors, or books on household medicine. And since so many items were published recently, they can often be found when heirs sell the library of a doctor or scientist.

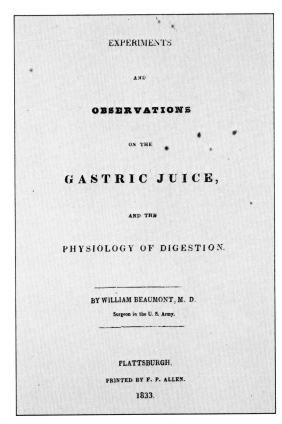

William Beaumont's work on human digestion was a scientific milestone. An Army surgeon, Beaumont treated a man wounded in the stomach and observed gastric mechanisms through the wound.

Nineteenth Century Classics

There is little point in a collector today setting out to accumulate important first editions of Elizabethan or even 18th Century works of literature. Wealthy collectors of the past bought up the most valuable items—such as editions of William Shakespeare, John Milton and Dr. Samuel Johnson—and usually bequeathed their magnificent collections to various libraries and museums.

Classics of the 19th Century are much more readily available, however. The increasingly literate public of that time bought thousands of copies of the works of their favorite authors. A great many volumes still lie in the dust of attics and closets. So it makes sense to aim at assembling the works of such popular 19th Century English novelists as Charles Dickens, William Thackeray or Anthony Trollope, or such American poets as Henry Wadsworth Longfellow or John Greenleaf Whittier.

Adding spice to the pursuit of most 19th Century novelists is the fact that their works appeared in several different forms. First came "parts": the novels were initially issued in monthly installments, usually about 20 of them. After the final monthly part had been published, the subscribers often had them gathered, sewn together and bound in cloth. Collectors refer to these as the first edition in book form. Advertisements were printed in the front and back sections of each part, and for the collectors of today the most desirable sets have all of the ads intact.

Then there was another kind of first edition, bound in paper covers. Known as wrappers, these covers carry the title and often illustrations of the story, as well as advertisements. They were the paperback books of their time, and were purchased by the hundreds of thousands. They were taller and narrower than today's paperbacks and much more densely printed, in small type and with the lines close together.

Then came the regular first edition, a comparatively elegant production, usually in three volumes: readers in that pretelevision age demanded that favorites such as Dickens write long, triple-barreled novels.

Many Victorian first editions, including the original part works, have been found in American homes. English authors were immensely popular in the United States during the 19th Century. While the monthly parts of a Dickens novel were appearing, crowds used to gather on the New York City piers when a steamer from England was expected to dock, each person hoping to be

A Sir Walter Scott first edition is bound in three volumes—as were most long novels by English writers of the 19th Century.

the first to buy the most recent part of a current serial. Of course the odds are that those old volumes stashed away in the attic are second or third editions, or later editions that were printed in America. But valuable first editions sometimes do turn up. The best way to check is to refer to the author's bibliography.

Other fruitful places to look for 19th Century first editions of books by classic authors are at the sales periodically sponsored by college alumni groups (the Bryn Mawr bookshops and book sales that are held in various parts of the country are deservedly well known), by friends of libraries and by church organizations. These charity sales are so frequently rewarding because many of the members of these literate organizations contribute to the sale by thoroughly cleaning out the family bookshelves, and first editions are sometimes included among their donations. Charity book sales of this sort are usually advertised in the local newspaper.

Just as British classic books of the 19th Century are to be found in the United States, American first editions sometimes are discovered in England. British publishing firms frequently printed volumes written by American authors even before the American editions came off the presses. *The Whale,* published in London in 1851, is actually the first edition of Herman Melville's *Moby Dick,* which was published in New York later in the same year.

In general, first editions of works by popular American writers have been obtainable even from bookdealers for less than $50. This is true of Hawthorne's work, for example, or Longfellow's. The price varies, as always, with the book's condition, and it is advisable to purchase the cleanest copies.

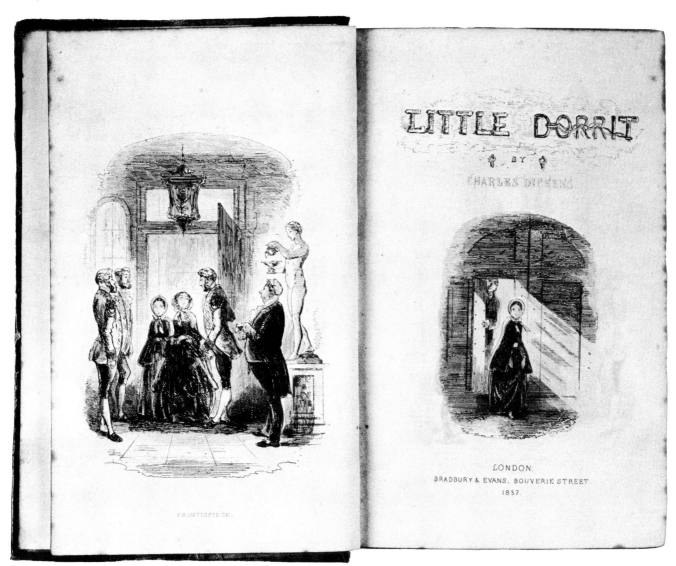

Numerous illustrations by Hablot K. Browne, who signed himself Phiz, form the frontispiece and enliven the title page of the first edition of Charles Dickens' "Little Dorrit." Most Victorian novels were illustrated; Phiz's drawings are among the most famous.

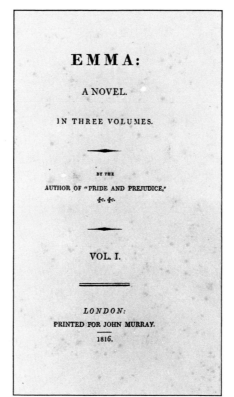

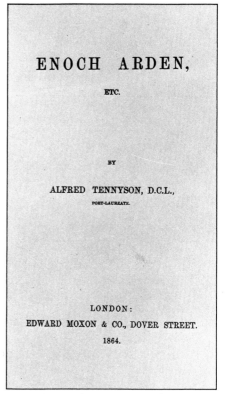

Most sought-after of 19th Century books are first editions of the poems of Lord Byron.

The title page of Jane Austen's 1816 novel "Emma" omits the diffident author's name.

First editions of Tennyson's works are popular among collectors of Victorian poetry.

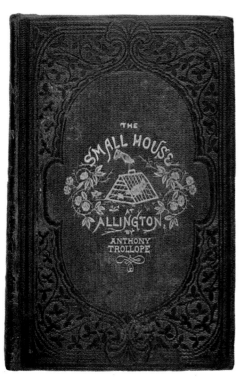

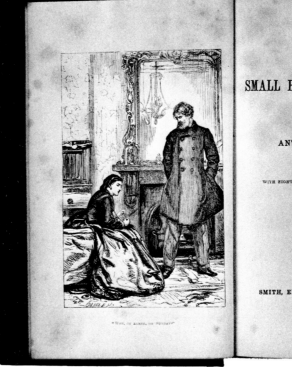

Illustrations by Sir John Everett Millais, a painter famous in the late 19th Century, add value to the first edition of "The Small House at Allington," one of the many works of Victorian novelist Anthony Trollope. The novel's ornate cover is shown at left, above.

THE

SONG OF HIAWATHA.

BY

HENRY WADSWORTH LONGFELLOW.

BOSTON:
TICKNOR AND FIELDS.
M DCCC LV.

American classic authors of the 19th Century include Longfellow, whose 1855 "Song of Hiawatha" was immensely popular.

THE

SCARLET LETTER,

A ROMANCE.

BY

NATHANIEL HAWTHORNE.

BOSTON:
TICKNOR, REED, AND FIELDS.
M DCCC L.

The title page of "The Scarlet Letter" contains the words "A Romance"—Nathaniel Hawthorne refused to call his tales novels.

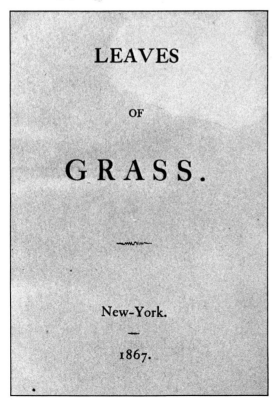

This title page of Walt Whitman's "Leaves of Grass," dated 1867, is the fourth of 12 versions, each slightly different.

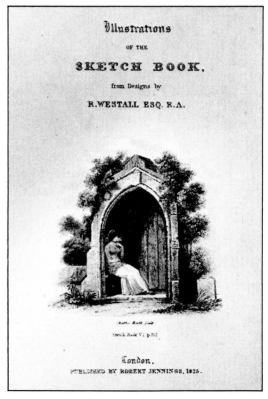

The London-published illustrations for American author Washington Irving's "Sketch Book" attest to his popularity abroad.

Press Books

A few craftsmen dedicated to the arts of typography and printing have made beautiful books from the time printing began. But the real interest in press books—especially handsome books that are run off in limited editions—dates back to the late 19th Century. The pioneer publisher in the press-book field was the Kelmscott Press, which was founded by the English poet and reformer William Morris in 1891. Morris' beautiful volumes, and especially his great edition of the writings of Chaucer, have influenced nearly all of the publishers doing fine editions in the 20th Century. The Kelmscott Press editions are valuable today; only a few are available for less than $200. One of the first 46 copies of Morris' Chaucer, bound in white pigskin, was sold for $10,630 in 1975.

Press books are usually not original publications, but rather reprinted standard works—the Greek and Roman classics, the works of Shakespeare and Dante, the poems of Edmund Spenser—or seldom-reprinted, minor works of both famous and not-so-famous authors. The pressruns are usually small, around 300 copies, perhaps, with a maximum printing of 2,000 copies. Many of these limited editions are illustrated by distinguished artists, and frequently the artist signs all of the copies; so does the author if he is living. A celebrated example is The Limited Editions Club's version of *Ulysses*, written by James Joyce, which includes illustrations by the French painter Henri Matisse. Matisse signed all 1,500 copies of this edition; Joyce signed 250 of them.

Press books are published by private presses, so called because they distribute books outside the normal channels used by other publishers. Sales are generally not made through regular bookstores, but only to subscribers, by mail, or through selected bookdealers. A supply of press books reaches the shops of rare-book dealers at times when the libraries of earlier collectors are broken up and sold off.

The best way to start a collection of press books, then, is to locate dealers who specialize in them, and to subscribe to private presses, such as The Limited Editions Club, that are still producing volumes of fine quality. Some of the press books to keep an eye out for in dealers' shops, or at auctions or other sales, are those that are produced by England's Ashendene, Vale and Daniel presses and those made in the United States by Mosher Press (founded in 1891) and Merrymount Press (founded in 1893). A press book, to be of any appreciable value, must be maintained in excellent condition—as nearly untouched as possible.

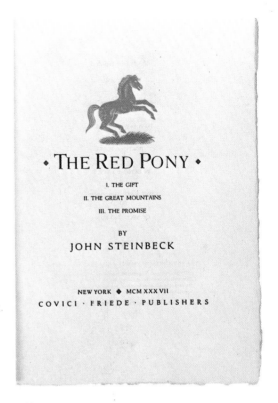

Only 699 copies were printed of the first edition of John Steinbeck's short novel "The Red Pony"; each was signed by the author.

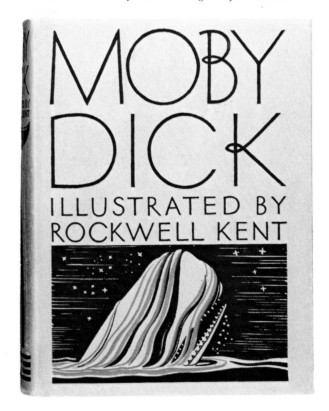

Rockwell Kent's dramatic picture of the white whale adorns the cover of an illustrated edition of Herman Melville's "Moby Dick."

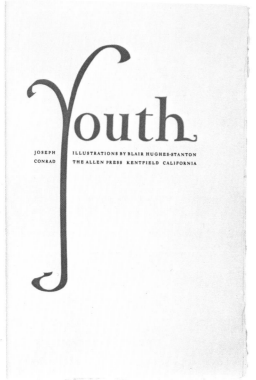

Unusual typography distinguishes the cover of a press-book edition of Joseph Conrad's novel "Youth" (above). The interior pages (right) contain woodcuts by Blair Hughes-Stanton. This edition, limited to 140 copies, was printed by the Allen Press in 1959.

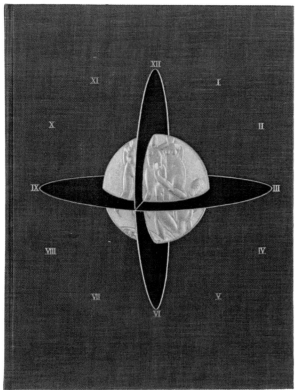

The cover design of The Limited Editions Club's "Ulysses" (above), illustrated by Henri Matisse, evokes the hours of the day, a motif in the novel's structure. Both Joyce's and Matisse' signatures appear on the colophon page of the book, of which 1,500 copies were printed.

Modern American First Editions

Collecting modern American first editions is an extremely popular field because these books are so available and are often such bargains. Some bookdealers do not realize that a novel only a few decades old may be highly valued by collectors. So modern American first editions are apt to turn up in the "out-of-print novels" section of secondhand bookstores.

This area of book collecting is usually thought of as including works of fiction or poetry by American writers published in the 20th Century. But most collectors stretch the period to include significant works published in the latter portion of the 19th Century. Pat Magarick, an international-insurance attorney who is active in this field, began his collection with the works of Mark Twain. Twain's first book appeared in 1867, and he was still being published up to the year of his death in 1910. Magarick's collection also includes first editions of such 20th Century American writers as Hemingway, Steinbeck, O'Neill and Sinclair Lewis.

"I got interested in collecting first editions," Magarick recalls, "by visiting old bookshops in Philadelphia, where I was a student in the '30s, and listening to collectors talk about authors such as Sherwood Anderson, William Faulkner, Ernest Hemingway and Scott Fitzgerald, who were then coming into fame and were already collected. I gradually picked my own authors to collect, writers whose style I admired. I've always bought first editions of writers I like through the years, and I'm still doing it."

Personal taste for an author's writing, most collectors agree, is the reason for building a collection. Various authorities have drawn up lists of collectible authors, writers whose works seem sure to remain in critical and popular favor—and to remain valuable. One such list is *High Spots of American Literature* by Merle Johnson, which includes many 20th Century writers. But his list is simply one bookman's choice of books whose fame will last.

Some collectors of modern American first editions specialize in the books that have won the annual Pulitzer Prize for the novel or drama. This group includes many books still famous, such as Thornton Wilder's *The Bridge of San Luis Rey* and Margaret Mitchell's *Gone with the Wind,* but it also includes many nearly forgotten books, such as Josephine Johnson's *Now in November,* the prize-winning novel in 1935. Other collectors concentrate on "schools" of writing, such as the Beat poets of the 1950s,

The first edition of Mark Twain's 1883 "Life on the Mississippi" is bound in decorated cloth; no dust jackets existed when it was printed.

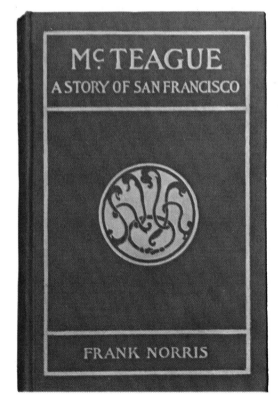

Frank Norris' "McTeague" (1899), although seldom read by the public, is a sought-after first among collectors of American fiction.

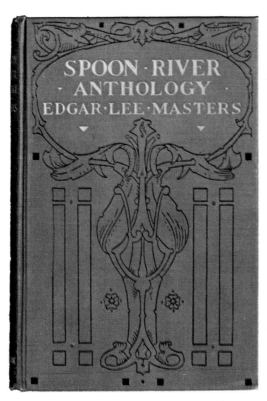

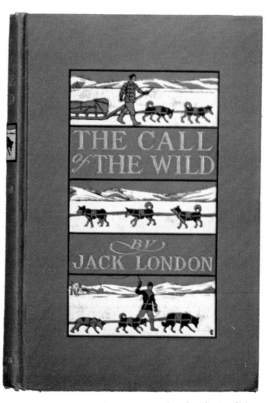

Edgar Lee Masters' free-verse "Spoon River Anthology"—first edition 1915—still evokes the flavor of small-town life.

Illustrations stamped on the cover make the first edition of Jack London's novel of the Klondike unusually decorative.

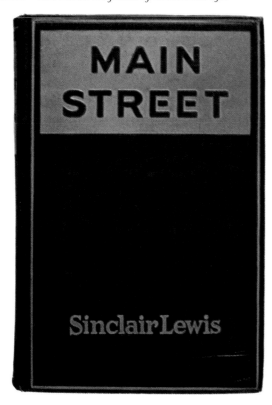

First editions of Sinclair Lewis' "Main Street," published in 1920, are rather rare, although the novel was later reprinted 29 times.

Steinbeck's "The Grapes of Wrath" appeared after dust jackets had become common. In mint condition, they increase the book's value.

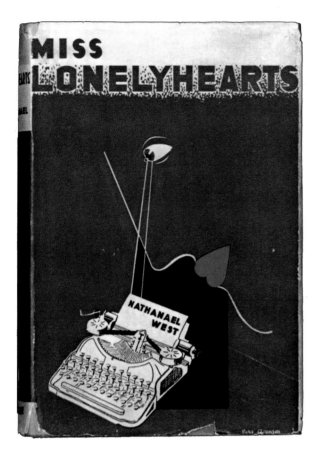

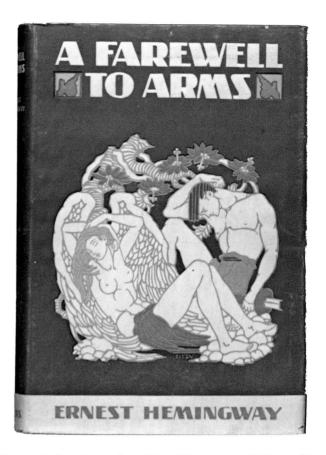

Firsts of "Miss Lonelyhearts" are difficult to find; the publisher issued only 2,000 copies of the initial edition of West's novel.

This jacket is from the regular edition of Hemingway's "A Farewell to Arms," which also appeared in a limited edition (opposite).

and limit their acquisitions to the works of such authors as Allen Ginsberg and Lawrence Ferlinghetti.

Beginners have sometimes thought that it would be simple to build a collection of valuable modern first editions by buying bestsellers as they came along and preserving them carefully. This approach also has pitfalls. One collector bought copies of the top novels of each year for 20 years. When he came to sell his untouched, immaculate collection, a few books, such as several by Hemingway, sold for 10 or 20 times their issue price. Others—the majority—were unsalable. The collection as a whole was a financial loss.

One of the key categories in modern firsts is limited, signed first editions. These have been issued since the 1920s for a number of American writers, among them Sherwood Anderson, Pearl Buck, John Steinbeck, Tennessee Williams, Eugene O'Neill, John Updike and Joseph Heller. Some are the beautifully designed, special press books discussed on page 112, but most are first editions printed from the same plates as the ordinary trade edition. They are produced on better paper, with better binding and nearly always in slipcase. Almost without exception limited editions, which are always numbered, have been signed by the author. A typical

limitation is 250 copies. The issue price of limited firsts has varied over the years, but their appreciation in many cases has been extraordinary. The limited edition of Hemingway's *A Farewell to Arms,* which sold for around $10 when it was published in 1929, was commanding $500 a half century later.

Even more than most book collectors, those who acquire modern first editions are concerned, almost fanatically so, about the physical condition of their books. Since only a handful of these books are extremely rare and copies of most can be acquired fairly easily, pristine condition is an important measure of value. And for a copy to appreciate in value, it should be virtually untouched. Special emphasis is placed on the dust jacket, one of the indispensables of modern book collecting. The dust jacket must be in fine condition, as free of chips or wear around edges as possible.

Fine copies of limited editions should be left untouched. One collector, hearing that it was necessary to have the dust jackets on modern first editions, built up at considerable expense a collection of books in their original jackets, which he carefully taped to the books. As he found when he tried to sell the collection, his use of tape had sacrificed virtually his entire investment.

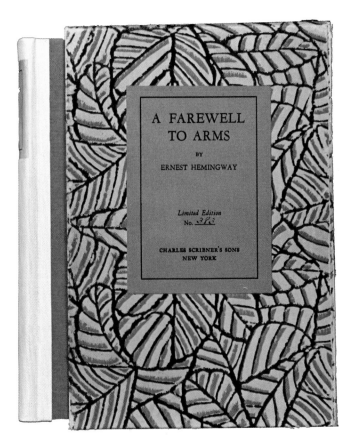

The limited edition of "A Farewell to Arms," published simultaneously with the regular one, has a different binding, and has a slipcase rather than a dust jacket. Each of the 510 copies was signed by the author and numbered (below). Copies of this limited edition have increased enormously in value since the book appeared in 1929.

THIS EDITION IS LIMITED TO FIVE
HUNDRED AND TEN COPIES OF WHICH
FIVE HUNDRED ARE FOR SALE AND
TEN FOR PRESENTATION

No. 383

Ernest Hemingway

LIBRARIES
Henry E. Huntington Library
San Marino, California 91108

Newberry Library
Chicago, Illinois 60610

The New York Public Library
New York, New York 10018

The Pierpont Morgan Library
New York, New York 10016

PERIODICALS
AB Bookman's Weekly, A B Bookman Publications, Inc., Clifton, New Jersey 07015

The American Book Collector, Arlington Heights, Illinois 60005

American Book-Prices Current, Columbia University Press, New York, New York 10027

BOOKS
Bennett, Whitman, *A Practical Guide to American Book Collecting (1663-1940)*. The Bennett Book Studios, Inc., 1941.

Garrison, Fielding and Leslie Morton, *Garrison and Morton's Medical Bibliography*. Grafton and Co., 1954.

Gee, Ernest, *Early American Sporting Books Seventeen Thirty-Four to Eighteen Forty-Four*. Haskell, 1928.

Howes, Wright, *U.S.iana, 1650-1950*. R. R. Bowker Co., 1962.

Johnson, Fridolf, *A Treasury of Bookplates from the Renaissance to the Present*. Dover Publications, Inc., 1977.

Johnson, Merle De Vore:
American First Editions. Mark Press, 1965.
High Spots of American Literature. Jenkins Publishing Co., 1969.

Lepper, Gary M., *A Bibliographical Introduction to Modern American Authors*. Serendipity Press, 1975.

Randall, David and John T. Winterich, *Primer of Book Collecting*. Crown Publishers, Inc., 1966.

Ransom, Will, *Private Presses & Their Books*. AMS Press, 1976.

Tannen, Jack, *How to Identify and Collect American First Editions*. Arco Publishing Co., Inc., 1976.

Toomey, Alice, ed., *World Bibliography of Bibliographies 1964-1974*. Rowman, 1977.

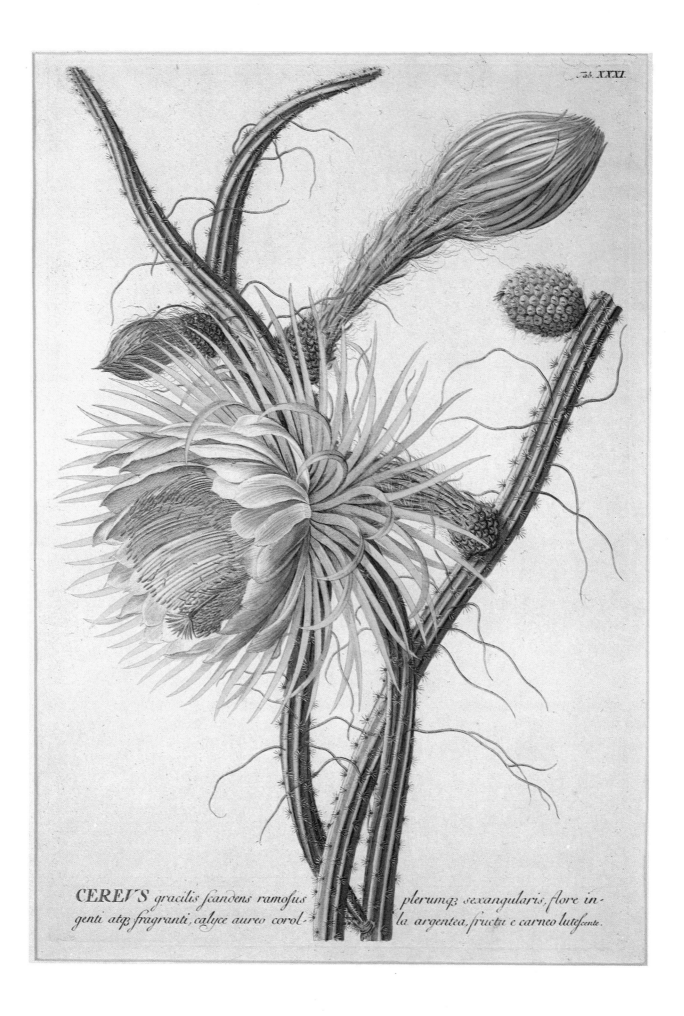

Tab. XXXI.

CEREVS *gracilis scandens ramosus*   *plerumq̃ sexangularis, flore in-*
genti atq̃ fragranti, calyce aureo corol-   *la argentea, fructu e carneo lutescente.*

Botanical Prints
A Merger of Science and Art

A bargain we discovered at a charity show in 1970 lured us into our hobby. Then, we knew little about botanical prints, but we could not resist two nicely framed pictures—a water lily *(page 125)* and a yellow gentian—priced at only $20 each even though they were 200 years old. Our prints were not identified, but later, in a rare-book store, we chanced upon prints very similar to ours. They were illustrations in an 18th Century book by the Italian Giorgio Bonelli. So at last our first acquisitions had a pedigree.

This discovery whetted our appetites for more prints of plants and more information about them. We began a serious study of this subject, which combines art, medi-

---

Joan Theobald, a research biologist, and her husband James, an engineer, have accumulated about 180 botanical prints and nearly 30 books containing information on their hobby.

---

cine, science and history, and provides a record of mankind's gradual acquisition of knowledge about plants and their uses, particularly in medicine.

Until the 15th Century, doctors got most of their information on medicinal properties of plants from hearsay and from Greek and Roman manuscripts. Some of these manuscripts contained drawings, in which plants were depicted clearly and realistically; the same naturalism was not achieved again for 1,000 years. All through the Middle Ages and the early Renaissance, most botanical manuscripts—and their drawings—were copies of earlier works. This practice resulted in pictures so formalized that the plants are almost unrecognizable.

But the late Renaissance brought changes. Botanical drawings became more accurate when prominent artists—among them Leonardo da Vinci and Albrecht Dürer—began drawing plants from direct observation. Simultaneously, the introduction of the printing press made it possible to produce texts with illustrations in multiple copies for wide circulation. It is the illustrations in such printed treatises—mechanical reproductions of one kind or another of the artist's original drawings—

The night-blooming Cereus at left is a hand-colored engraving that is based on an illustration by Georg Ehret, the most famous botanical artist of the 18th Century.

that are collectible botanical prints. Collectors seek out the works of famous artists who made the drawings, or of notable specialists who converted the drawings into forms that could be printed. Particularly desirable are prints associated with men who pioneered new and valuable techniques, advancing the art.

The early botanical books are called herbals. The first of importance, in the opinion of many collectors, is *Herbarum Vivae Eicones (Living Portraits of Plants),* published in Strasbourg, Germany, in 1530. It was written by a physician named Otto Brunfels and was illustrated by woodcuts of drawings by Hans Weiditz. We do not own any prints by Weiditz but we do own several from the same period that were published by Leonhart Fuchs.

Early in the 17th Century, artists began using two new techniques that enabled them to delineate features of plants more exactly: engraving and etching. Two of our favorite prints are engravings that illustrate Robert's *Recueil des Plants (Collection of Plants),* first published in 1701. Most of the drawings for this volume are by Nicolas Robert, an artist famous for his delicate flower prints. But Robert died in 1685, before the work was completed, and some of the plates were done by the much-admired artist and engraver, Louis de Châtillon.

During the 17th Century, as plants began to be appreciated for their beauty as well as their utility, another sort of botanical publication became popular: the florilegium, or flower book, consisting solely of pictures. Probably the most famous is *The Temple of Flora,* written and published in the late 18th Century by an English doctor, Robert John Thornton. The book's hand-colored illustrations of plants, done by various artists and engravers, are set against romantic landscape backgrounds, in contrast to the previous practice of omitting backgrounds.

But the most renowned botanical publication of the 18th Century is undoubtedly Carolus Linnaeus' *Species Plantarum (Species of Plants),* published in 1753. Linnaeus' system for classifying plants, followed in essence to this day, was quickly adopted for many books whose illustrations were pre-Linnaean but that were reissued with Linnaean names. This can be confusing for collectors, but a handy publication, Otto Stapf's 1929 *Index Londinensis (page 129),* available in many botanical reference libraries, lists the sources of most plant illustrations

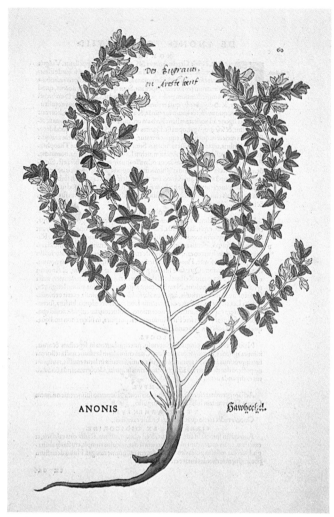

A pheasant's eye, from Leonhart Fuchs's 16th Century "De Historia Stirpium," labels the plant in Latin and German. Fuchs's book was so popular it went into 35 editions—and was widely pirated.

This cross section of a lemon is from "Hesperides," printed in Rome in 1646. The legend on the ribbon at the top describes the fruit, native to Liguria in northwest Italy, as spongy and warty-skinned.

published after Linnaeus' book. While these changes were occurring in botanical science, one botanical illustrator preempted the field in art. He was a German, Georg Dionysius Ehret, who is thought to have provided as many as 500 illustrations for the early volumes of an eight-volume *Phytanthoza Iconographia (Illustrated Record of Flowering Plants),* which began publication in 1737.

At the turn of the 19th Century, a noted school of botanical artists flourished in France. Its best-known member was Pierre-Joseph Redouté, one of whose prints is reproduced on page 128. Other important 19th Century artists are the Bauer brothers, Ferdinand and Francis, and the less important but popular Pancrace Bessa and William Baxter.

Collectors rarely come across more than one print at a time by a famous artist, and when they do, the price can be discouraging. Some plates by Redouté, for instance,

were selling for more than $100 in the late 1970s. However, collectors can easily find modestly priced works by lesser-known artists of the 19th Century—when botanical prints reached their height of popularity—and by contemporary botanical artists. They can also find copies of antique prints at reasonable prices, but they should be wary of reproductions sold as originals.

Most reproductions are marked with a printer's symbol or legend *(page 127)* that identifies them as copies. They can also be recognized by the reproduction process: modern copies produced photomechanically by widely used printing techniques reveal a pattern of dots

The accuracy with which such detail as roots were depicted by Louis Châtillon, who was both artist and engraver for this 1701 French print, makes his work especially desirable. The plant is alchemilla, or lady's-mantle, once believed capable of restoring feminine beauty.

Alchimilla vulgaris CB.pin 319.

Pied de Lion, *ou* Alchimille.

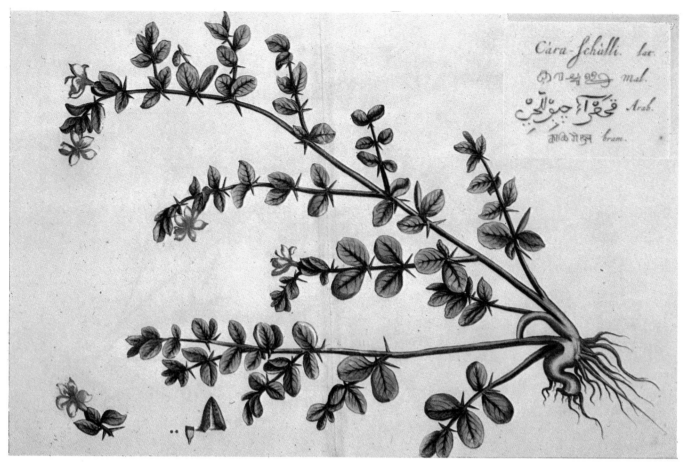

Cara-fchúlli. *lat.*
ⓐⓝⓢ mal.
فَقْفَرآحِوۡلُٱلۡجِين Arab.
ब्रह्मेत्तु bram.

Barleria buxifolia is one of the plants portrayed in "Hortus Indicus Malabaricus," devoted to flora of the Dutch colony of Malabar in *India and published in the late 17th Century. The plant's name is at the upper right in Latin, Malabarese, Arabic and Brahmin.*

under a magnifier. Copies made by creating new etchings in the old style can be harder to detect but are often marked in some way as reproductions. The book *How Prints Look* by W. M. Ivins Jr. *(page 129)* is invaluable in distinguishing new prints from old. Among genuine antique prints, the most expensive are the easiest to authenticate: many of the prints by important artists were inscribed at the lower left with their names. A hand lens can help in examining prints for these names as well as printers' marks and printing method.

Novice collectors can find many places—from thrift shops to posh galleries—to buy original prints. Sometimes the hardest part of the search is making a shopkeeper understand what you need. Do not give up if an initial request for books of prints on natural history is met with a blank stare; try asking for prints from books on gardening, horticulture or even animals. Better print shops, of course, have drawers marked "Botany."

Even reputable dealers may be ill-informed. We once bought four prints identified as coming from Johann Weinmann's *Phytanthoza,* but although they resembled Weinmann's prints, we did not believe they were au-

thentic. With the help of experts who have assisted us several times, we determined that the prints were from G. W. Knorr's *Thesaurus,* published in Germany in 1780.

In many cities collectors can get information on prints from print clubs and antique associations, whose members are often willing to share what they know. Members of the Guild of Natural Science Illustrators *(page 129)* receive a monthly newsletter that lists scheduled exhibits and discusses the work of contemporary artists. By collecting art-show catalogues, collectors keep abreast of available works. Some even track down contemporary artists through museums and galleries showing their work; the collectors then deal with the artists directly.

As much attention should be given to the maintenance of botanical prints as to their acquisition, because the value of a piece can be drastically diminished by improper care. When handling a print, lift it with both hands, to keep it from bending. Never touch the printed

A plate depicting Butcher's broom, from a botanical book produced in the 18th Century in England by Timothy Sheldrake, is notable for its lengthy description of the plant and its use as a diuretic.

BUTCHER'S BROOM.

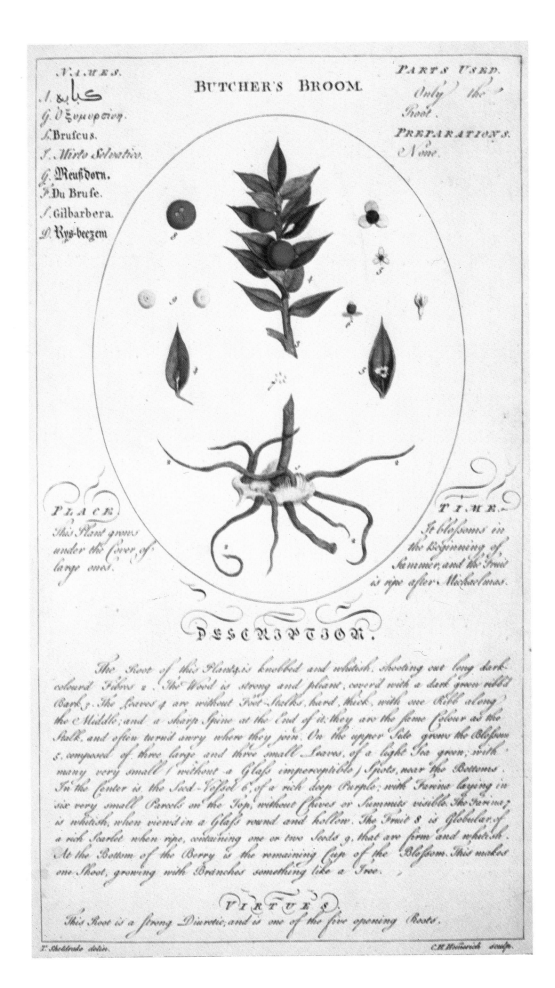

NAMES.

A. بسبا‎

G. ὀ Ξυμυρσιη.

L. Bruscus.

I. Mirto Selvatico.

G. Meusdorn.

F. Du Bruse.

S. Gilbarbera.

D. Rys-beezem

PARTS USED.

Only the Root.

PREPARATIONS.

None.

PLACE

This Plant grows under the Cover of large ones.

TIME.

It blossoms in the Beginning of Summer, and the Fruit is ripe after Michaelmas.

DESCRIPTION.

The Root of this Plant, is knobbed and whitish, shooting out long dark coloured Fibres 2. The Wood is strong and pliant, cover'd with a dark green ribb'd Bark 3. The Leaves 4 are without Foot-Stalks, hard, thick, with one Ribb along the Middle; and a sharp Spine at the End of it; they are the same Colour as the Stalk, and often turn'd awry where they join. On the upper Side grows the Blossom 5, composed of three large and three small Leaves, of a light Sea green, with many very small (without a Glass imperceptible) Spots, near the Bottoms. In the Center is the Seed-Vessel 6, of a rich deep Purple; with Farine laying in six very small Parcels on the Top, without Chives or Summits visible. The Farine is whitish, when view'd in a Glass round and hollow. The Fruit 8 is Globular, of a rich Scarlet when ripe, containing one or two Seeds 9, that are firm and whitish. At the Bottom of the Berry is the remaining Cup of the Blossom. This makes one Shoot, growing with Branches something like a Tree.

VIRTUES.

This Root is a strong Diuretic; and is one of the five opening Roots.

T. Sheldrake delin.

C.H. Hemerich sculp.

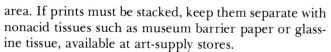

A common sneezewort (above), powdered and snuffed in the 1700s, was drawn by James Sowerby in a book on London flora.

Contrary to custom, a diseased plant—an almond branch—is portrayed (right) in an early-19th Century French book.

area. If prints must be stacked, keep them separate with nonacid tissues such as museum barrier paper or glassine tissue, available at art-supply stores.

Good matting will protect prints, but the wrong kind can cause damage. Almost all colored matboards and wood backing boards contain acid, which will produce a brown stain and eventually destroy the paper. Only nonacid matting board and backing board made entirely of cotton or rag should come into contact with the print.

Special gummed papers such as white linen tape are available for attaching the top edge of a print to the backing board. The hinges made to mount stamps in albums are a handy substitute. Ordinary household glues and pressure-sensitive tapes such as cellophane or masking tape should never be used, and heat-sensitive photo-mounting tissue also should be avoided. A final concern is the environment in which prints are kept. Good air circulation should be maintained where prints are stored and humidity should stay below 75 per cent to prevent foxing, a brown stain caused by mold that thrives in higher humidity. Fluctuations and extremes of temperature should be avoided, as should exposure to direct sunlight or fluorescent light, unless the fluorescent tubes are the special kind used by museums.

For related material, see the articles on Currier and Ives, Prints, and Wildlife Prints in separate volumes.

This primitive rendering of a water lily—the authors' first print—is from an 18th Century work, Giorgio Bonelli's "Hortus Romanus."

Tab. 57.

Nymphoides aquis innatans. I.R.H. 153. — *Ital.* *Ninfea minore*

Pinus microcarpa

Ferdinand Bauer drew the art for this print of a pine tree for an English book published early in the 19th Century.

Prints from a Periodical

An unusual—and economical—source of fine botanical prints is a periodical, *Botanical Magazine,* published semiannually in London since 1787. It was the first periodical to provide amateur gardeners with horticultural information, and its quick acceptance by the public inspired half a dozen imitations around the turn of the 19th Century; none survived and *Botanical Magazine* soon resumed its solitary eminence.

From its inception through the first half of the 19th Century, the magazine printed excellent engravings, which were colored by hand in every copy. After engravings became too expensive to produce, they were replaced by lithographs, also individually hand colored, until 1948 when modern color-printing techniques supplanted the handwork.

Many of the 9,688 hand-colored prints published in *Botanical Magazine* can be found nowadays in antique-print stores or bookstores, often at reasonable prices. Antique dealers who are unfamiliar with the prints sometimes sell them for as little as $5 to $10 apiece.

This lithograph of a morning glory was made for an 1847 issue of "Botanical Magazine" by Walter Hood Fitch, the publication's sole artist for four decades.

This detail from the carnation picture at right—originally published in 1613—identifies the print as a modern reproduction made recently by Edizioni Ponte Vecchio in Italy. Most such copies bear similar marks to indicate they are not originals.

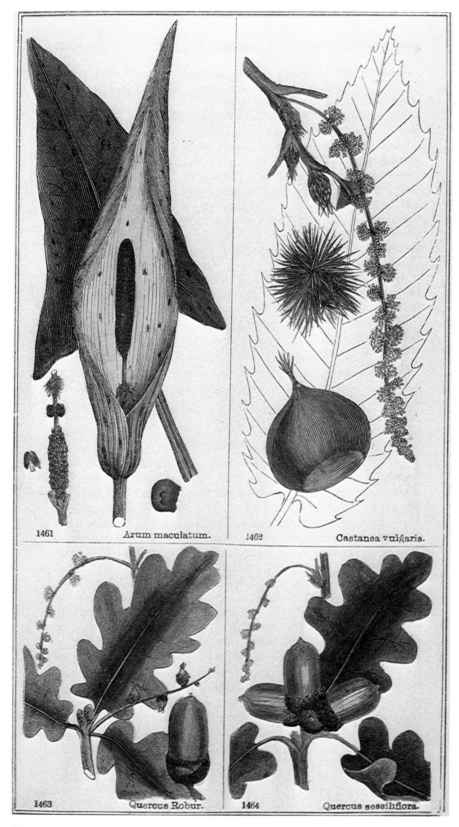

1461   Arum maculatum.

1462   Castanea vulgaris.

1463   Quercus Robur.

1464   Quercus sessiliflora.

Pictures were arranged four to a page to economize on paper in "Florigraphia Britannica." The four-volume set by a physician named Richard Deakin was published from 1837 to 1848. The plants on this page are, clockwise from top left, cuckoopint, chestnut and two kinds of oak.

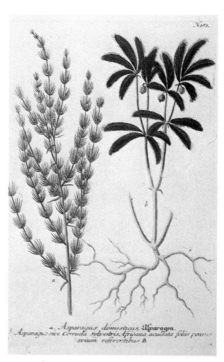

A print of asparagus is from Johann Weinmann's "Phytanthoza Iconographia." The book came out in 1737, but many editions were produced and prints are easy to find.

This print, after a drawing by Pierre-Joseph Redouté, costs $40 or less, the prints from his books on roses and lilies up to $500.

Prized Prints of Today

Many collectors feel that esthetics are as important as age or rarity, and they seek out unusual botanical prints made today, particularly those done by modern techniques such as silk screen or linoleum-block printing. Notable are the prints of Henry Evans and Henry Mockel, both Californians. In samples of their work at right, the simplicity of Evans' California poppies contrasts with Mockel's desert flower, for which he used 30 silk screens. The depth and shading produced by so many stencils often cause Mockel's work to be taken for watercolors.

Henry Evans' linoleum-block print of poppies and a brodiaea (left) and Henry Mockel's silk screen of a ghostflower were made in the 1970s.

The French artist Pancrace Bessa drew the illustration for this engraving of wisteria, a plant imported to France from China, in his "Flore des Jardiniers," published in Paris in 1836.

LIBRARIES
Hunt Institute for Botanical Documentation
Pittsburgh, Pennsylvania 15213

The National Agricultural Library
Beltsville, Maryland 20705

PERIODICALS
GNSI Newsletter, Guild of Natural Science Illustrators, Washington, D.C. 20044

Print Collectors' Newsletter, New York, New York 10021.

BOOKS
Blunt, Wilfred, *The Art of Botanical Illustration.* Collins, 1967.

Bush-Brown, Louise, *Men with Green Pens: Lives of the Great Writers on Plants in Early Times.* Dorrance & Company, 1964.

Ivins, W. M., *How Prints Look.* Beacon Press, Inc., 1958.

Stapf, Otto, *Index Londinensis.* Royal Horticultural Society of London, 1929. (Supplement published 1941.)

Zigrosser, Carl and Christa M. Gaehde, *A Guide to the Collecting and Care of Original Prints.* Crown Publishers, Inc., 1965.

Bottles
Containers That Outlive Their Contents

Successful collectors of antique bottles combine the instincts of an archeologist with the sharp-eyed persistence of a private detective. One I know was once leafing through a newspaper when he spotted a report that the owners of the town's oldest hotel, a pair of elderly spinsters, were selling out and moving to Florida. My friend telephoned to ask the spinsters if they had any old bottles. The answer was no, but it seemed incredible that a hotel 140 years old contained not one single piece of antique glassware. So he drove over and offered to clean up the cellar and attic for the two old ladies. There was nothing in the attic, but one corner of the cellar was crammed with wine and medicine bottles, many dating from the 19th Century. In return for half a day's labor, my friend

Orthodontist Burton Spiller began collecting bottles in 1962 when he saw a barrel-shaped container for patent medicine at a flea market. He now has one of the most representative collections in the country.

walked off with hundreds of dollars worth of rarities.

What my friend was searching for—what all American bottle collectors seek—were bottles made between 1810 and 1910, the heyday of bottlemaking in the United States. Before 1810 few glass containers were manufactured in the United States; after 1910 most bottles were machine made. Nineteenth Century bottles, however, were formed by hand in a riotous variety of shapes, sizes and designs. The glass itself is interesting, usually greenish or bluish in color because of impurities, and frequently contains bubbles, surface irregularities and bits of stone. There are bottles shaped like log cabins, bananas, pigs and drums. Many whiskey bottles have bas-reliefs of Presidential candidates or other heroes molded in them. Bottles that contained the many dubious patent medicines of the time have the names of their products embossed on the glass, names like "The Cuticura System of Curing Constitutional Humors."

Choice items from the author's collection include green and blue soda- and mineral-water bottles (top), and colored patent-medicine bottles (middle row). The barrel-shaped vessels on the bottom shelf held the popular 19th Century nostrums called bitters.

Although old bottles can be purchased at auctions, in flea markets or from antique dealers, a great part of the fun for many bottle collectors is going on archeological field trips, searching in old farmhouses and barns, or even getting out a shovel and digging around for bottles in old dumps or cellar pits. It is one field of collecting in which interesting rarities can be found with virtually no cost except a little labor.

Among the rarities most sought by collectors are whiskey bottles with portraits of Presidents or other politicians embossed on their sides. These flasks were not just advertising; they were sometimes distributed among would-be voters at election time in the hope that inebriation would make them vote the right way. Non-Presidential worthies whose faces grace whiskey bottles include the Marquis de Lafayette *(page 134)* and Jenny Lind, the Swedish singer brought to the United States by P. T. Barnum *(page 135)*. Other bottles were decorated with patriotic symbols such as the American eagle. The rarest is the "Jared Spencer Bottle," an amber bottle embossed with a medallion bearing the likeness of the maker himself, Jared Spencer.

With the rise of 19th Century temperance movements, liquids called tonics became popular. They were supposed to be good for the health, and some might have been; what is undeniable is that nearly all were a polite substitute for whiskey. They were loaded with alcohol—some were 90 proof. The bottles they came in were embossed with brand names such as "Clemen's Indian Tonic," "Pure Family Nectar," and "Perry Davis' Pain-Killer." One, alcohol laden like the rest, was labeled "Dr. Beers, the Inebriate's Hope"—either a cynical suggestion that it cured drunkenness or a more plausible promise of hair-of-the-dog relief from hangover.

Closely allied to tonics were the so-called bitters. They were concoctions of evil-tasting herbs laced with enough alcohol to numb the symptoms of any ailment. Like tonics, they were supposed to be good for you, especially as "stomachics," remedies for digestive disorders. Bitters bottles are prized by collectors because they were made in a variety of shapes. Indian Queen Bitters came in a bottle shaped like the human body, Plantation Bitters in a glass log cabin, Dr. Fisch's bitters in a bottle shaped like

The two whiskey flasks on the left above have handles to facilitate drinking straight from the bottle, a widespread custom in the 19th

Century. Both of these flasks have the distillers' names embossed on the glass; the simpler flask at right does not.

The three glass containers above are also whiskey flasks dating from the era when saloons and liquor stores gave away samples in souvenir

bottles. The pig and pistol held a couple of ounces; the jolly fat man, 5 to 6 ounces. Such oddly shaped bottles are called figurals.

a fish (a pun on his name), McKeever's Army bitters in a drum-shaped bottle and Suffolk bitters in bottles resembling pigs. I began my collection with a barrel-shaped bottle embossed with the words "Hall's Bitters."

The wide sale of the alcoholic beverages called bitters and tonics reflects the primitive state of medicine in the 19th Century. On the other hand, more care seems to have been taken then than now with downright poisons. As early as 1872 the American Medical Association urged producers of poisons to use bottles having distinctive designs. Some of the resulting bottles are triangular or have hobnailed surfaces to make them instantly recognizable to fingers groping in the dark—or to people unable to read labels.

For variety of design, however, no bottles surpass those that were made to hold ink. Desk-sized ink bottles called individual inks were made in the shape of almost anything but ordinary bottles—ribbed umbrellas, igloos, bananas, cones, buildings and fantastic figures of men.

Collectors also value the handsome, if less imaginatively shaped, bottles that were part of the equipment of any self-respecting barbershop in the days when it was a male preserve and not a unisex styling salon. Much prized, too, are mineral-water bottles. Dozens of spas in the United States once bottled the water that bubbled up from their underground springs and embossed the spa name on the containers. Mineral-water bottles from such famous and long-popular sources as Poland Springs, Maine, and Saratoga Springs, New York, are relatively common. More valuable are older bottles from defunct spas or, since most mineral water came in greenish bottles, the less common ones of amber glass.

Some collectors prize glass objects that are not technically bottles at all. Among them are the glass candy containers that delighted 19th Century children (and are still made today). They were shaped like pistols, cars, boats and locomotives (page 145). Best of all were railroad lanterns, which were always filled with red candies.

Other collectible glass containers from the 19th Century include globes that, filled with carbon tetrachloride, were intended to be fire extinguishers. When a fire started, the globe was supposed to be thrown at the flames, where it would break, allowing its contents to extinguish the blaze. Since these grenades, as they were often called, were made in the era of ornate Victorian decoration, many were ornamental as well as useful, coming in a variety of colors and shapes. There were reds, greens, yellows and blues, and ovals, teardrops, barrels and spheres.

Other glass objects that were made to be destroyed were target balls. Because humane societies protested the use of live pigeons as targets at shooting contests, glassmakers in the 1850s devised small colored balls for the purpose. Filled with smoke or confetti and thrown in the air, they made satisfying marks for wing shots. Target balls were made of blue, green, amber or red glass, and many were embossed with decorative patterns. The invention of the clay pigeon in the 1880s doomed target balls, but some have survived the years—and the shooter's gun.

Although all these old glass containers may be found, like other collectibles, wherever antiques are on sale, many collectors prefer to make their hobby something of an outdoor sport. One bottle-collecting family haunts deserted mining camps and ghost towns in the West. They dig by the back doors of tumble-down saloons for old whiskey bottles, or in ravines where the miners might have dumped their trash. They also look under abandoned buildings or under floors, where bottle-laden litter might have been kicked. Ravines or depressions behind old hotels or summer resorts can also be rich with antique bottles. And so are sites closer to home. Bulldozers knocking down old city slums can unearth cellars and basements full of old glassware.

If you plan to engage in such amateur archeology, you must be aware of the rules. First, you need permission from the owner of the property—and all property, even seemingly public land beside a road, is owned by someone (or some government agency). And second, you must avoid interfering with scholarly historical research. Increasingly, the places you might dig for bottles are of interest to professional archeologists, who now are turning their attention to 19th and early-20th Century artifacts. They excavate according to a precise pattern to preserve identifying earth layers, which can be destroyed by the casual digging of novices. So before you set out, check with a local historical society or the archeological department of the nearest university to make sure your work will not block future discoveries.

Strenuous digging expeditions are not an essential part of bottle hunting; less athletic searching also pays off. One collector of old flasks, who has never lifted a spade in his life, goes to auctions exclusively. But his technique is to go to any auction where bottles might turn up. One winter he attended a house sale not far from his hometown. It was a modest auction, mostly old pots and pans and a few pieces of furniture. But in the presale viewing his sharp, trained eye lit on some old canning jars—and with them a historical flask. It was not just any historical flask, but a pint flask with President John Quincy Adams on one side and old Dr. Dyott, who had run the Dyottville, Pennsylvania, glassworks, on the other. The bottle dated from the first quarter of the 19th Century and was worth several hundred dollars.

When that box of bottles came up, the collector jumped in with a dollar bid. A lady in the audience wanted those bottles too; she needed them for canning. He had to go up to five dollars to get his Adams flask.

These "historical" whiskey flasks show the Marquis de Lafayette, the French officer who aided Washington during the Revolution. Among the U.S. Presidents who appear on similar flasks are John Quincy Adams, George Washington and William Henry Harrison.

A sunburst design, like the one above, was one of the earlier embossed motifs and was used by a number of glassworks until the 1870s.

The name of Jenny Lind, the popular 19th Century singer called the Swedish Nightingale, is misspelled on the blue flask above.

Flasks bearing embossed pictures of horse-drawn trains reflect the pride Americans took in their fast-developing transportation system in *the early 1800s. Sailing ships, sheaves of wheat and other symbols of American prosperity are found on other historical flasks.*

The medicine bottle at left is especially valuable because it is completely intact—it still has its original contents, seal and labeled box. It was made about 1880. The blue patent-medicine bottle below, which probably dates from the Civil War period, asserts confidently that its contents can be used to cure malaria.

A small blue bottle that once contained a poisonous substance has hobnailed sides to warn the unwary of its lethal contents. Poison bottles were made in such telltale shapes from the 1870s until 1930.

How to Date a Hand-blown Bottle

The age of an old bottle often can be determined by looking for marks on its sides or bottom resulting from certain steps in the manufacturing process. In the method generally used to make bottles before about 1850, a glass blower picked up on the end of a blowpipe a glob of molten glass and expanded it by blowing through the pipe. When the body of the bottle was shaped, he broke it free of the pipe to shape the neck. To hold the bottle while this was being done, an iron rod called a pontil was dipped into hot glass and affixed to the base of the vessel. After the neck and lip were finished the pontil was broken off, leaving a sharp, round "pontil scar" on the bottom *(below, center).*

Shortly before 1850 glassmakers began to use a "bare iron pontil"—they heated the pontil, which melted the bottom of the bottle enough to assure adhesion. Bottles made this way exhibit a circular black, red or white mark on the bottom from fragments of the oxidized iron *(below, right).* Then in the 1850s a clamp was developed that grasped the bottle securely without marring it. So most bottles made after 1860 show a smooth unscarred base.

Another guide to age is mold marks. Glass blowers had long shaped bottles in molds of metal or wood, as well as by hand, and the chronology of mold development left its record in markings on the glass. The earliest molds formed only the body; neck and lip were added by hand. Bottles made with pre-1860 molds show a ridge down each side of the body, but not all the way up the neck.

About 1860, most of a bottleneck could be shaped in molds, so the seam ran higher up the neck. In the late 1800s, the molds were modified to shape much of the lip. Mold marks then ran within ¼ inch of the bottle top. In 1903, there appeared the bottlemaking machine, which made a mold seam running over the top.

Some molded bottles show no seam marks. Between 1890 and 1910, the makers of tall wine bottles put a paste into their molds that made the insides slippery. They spun the bottles before removing them from the mold, erasing the seams. Many of these "turn-mold" bottles show tiny horizontal scratches caused by the spinning.

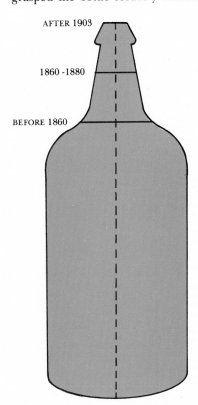

Molded bottles can be dated by observing the length of the seam left by the mold. The higher the seam, the later the bottle.

Early hand-blown bottles bear a "pontil scar" where the rod used to hold the bottle left behind a sharp-edged chunk of glass.

Bottles hand-blown between 1845 and 1870 have flecks of color on their bottoms deposited by a bare iron pontil.

The glass beer bottles at right above date from the mid-19th Century, when glass replaced stoneware (left) for beer containers. Many early beer bottles are embossed with decorations.

A green mineral-water bottle shows its age— Washington Springs is long defunct.

Soda bottles (above) have heavy glass walls to resist the gas pressure from their carbonated contents. Some, such as the one at left, have

rounded bottoms so that they cannot stand up, a position that would have allowed their cork stoppers to dry out and shrink.

Two condiment bottles bear the so-called cathedral style of decoration, with embossed designs resembling arches and vaulting.

The green milk bottle above is a rarity. Milk began to be bottled late in the 19th Century, when clear glass was in wide use.

Although the label reads "Banana Juice," this bottle's shape indicates that it was probably used for some kind of alcoholic beverage.

The embossed design on the bottle above resembles a drum. The bottle held bitters, a popular remedy that was as alcoholic as whiskey.

This bitters bottle in the shape of an Indian maiden reflects American belief in "Indian herb cures" during the late 19th Century.

Bitters bottles shaped like log cabins (left and center) hark to the 1840 Presidential campaign, when they were used to give a frontiers-man's image to the aristocratic William Henry Harrison. The spiral shape of the bitters bottle at right is a rare design.

The face of a cabaret entertainer enlivens a custom-decorated hair-tonic bottle that was used in a 19th Century barbershop.

A set of barbershop bottles, decorated with pictures of winsome females, recalls the day when every gentleman kept his own razor, lotion bottles and other tonsorial tools at his favorite barbershop. The bottles above contained hair tonics or after-shave lotions.

Ink bottles range in size from tiny containers 2 inches high for use on desks to quart and gallon "master inks" (right). Many of both sizes were embossed with the inkmaker's name, and desk types came in fanciful shapes, such as the ribbed "umbrella" at right, below.

The 2- to 3-ounce glass balls at right, used for target practice before clay pigeons were invented, are about 3 inches in diameter.

Glass fire extinguishers come in many shapes. When they were thrown at a fire they broke and released their liquid contents.

These antique candy containers are shaped like a lunch pail, a locomotive and an early automobile with driver and passenger.

MUSEUMS
The Bennington Museum
Bennington, Vermont 05201

The Corning Museum of Glass
Corning, New York 14830

Toledo Museum of Art
Toledo, Ohio 43697

COLLECTORS ORGANIZATIONS
Genesee Valley Bottle Collectors Association
P.O. Box 7528
West Ridge Station
Rochester, New York 14615

Iowa Antique Bottleers
1506 Albia Road
Ottumwa, Iowa 52501

Memphis Bottle Collectors Club
232 Tilton Road
Memphis, Tennessee 38111

The Pennsylvania Bottle Collectors Association
743 Woodberry Road
York, Pennsylvania 17403

San Jose Antique Bottle Collectors Society
P.O. Box 5432
San Jose, California 95150

Western Slope Bottle Club
Box 354
Palisade, Colorado 81526

PERIODICALS
Bottle News, Collector's Media, Inc.,
Kermit, Texas 79745

Old Bottle Magazine, Maverick Publications,
Bend, Oregon 97701

BOOKS
Ketchum, William C., Jr., *A Treasury of American Bottles.* The Bobbs-Merrill Company, Inc., 1975.

McKearin, George S. and Helen, *American Glass.* Crown Publishers, Inc., 1941. (Revised, 1948)

Munsey, Cecil, *The Illustrated Guide to Collecting Bottles.* Hawthorn Books, Inc., 1970.

Boxes
Ministorage in Many Forms

According to my dictionary, a box is "a rectangular container, typically having a lid or cover." The dictionary does not do justice to the subject. Boxes can be rectangular, but they can also be round, cylindrical, oval or many-sided, or they can be shaped like people, books, animals or fruit. And not all boxes have lids.

Nor does the dictionary mention size—and boxes can vary from the minuscule to those only a professional mover can move. My collection has visiting-card cases a fraction of an inch thick and perhaps 4 inches long, and, at the other extreme, 30-inch-high trunks. In between

---

Mary Mac Franklin, a former librarian, has found a use for every single one of the hundred boxes she and her husband have acquired on country antiquing jaunts.

---

are letter-writing cases a foot and a half wide, dressing-table boxes 4 inches long for a lady's face powder and even smaller vinaigrettes, boxes for a pungent vinegar mixture that the fastidious of an earlier age sniffed to mask unpleasant odors.

The dictionary also neglects to mention the wide variety of materials from which boxes have been made. Many, of course, are made of wood. But boxes have also been made from materials as diverse as gold and papier-mâché, silver and tree bark, marble and leather, copper and porcelain. The field of box collecting, then, is a large one, to say the least. The collector is free to range widely, acquiring any sort of boxlike container, or to specialize in one sort; even within a specialty the variety of shapes and decoration will be satisfyingly large.

Popular among collectors are small boxes, partly because they are easy to store and display, partly because they are found in such variety—vinaigrettes, calling-card cases, trinket boxes, stamp boxes and the myriad containers that were used for cosmetics. These small containers have been made for centuries of every material from lacquered wood to semiprecious stones.

At the opposite extreme are the large, often roughly made wooden boxes that in times past were essential household accessories. Housewives of earlier centuries bought staples in bulk and stored them at home—in boxes. Many were designed to be hung on the kitchen wall. Always hung there were candle boxes *(page 150)*, to keep mice from eating the tallow. There were tinder-boxes and Bible boxes *(page 153)*. Some of these utilitarian containers were handsome, decorated with charming primitive paintings or carvings. The best place for collectors to look for them is in antique shops that specialize in primitives or country antiques.

Closely allied to these household necessities are similar boxes made in specific regions, such as the Pennsylvania Dutch area of southeastern Pennsylvania. Here were made, for example, special boxes in which brides could keep their bridal caps, lace collars and other bits of finery *(page 152)*. These boxes are often decorated with figures and landscapes that have cheerful red, green, yellow, blue or (more sedately) brown backgrounds. The collector wanting such regional specialties will have the best luck, of course, in the region itself.

A fourth category of box includes more elegant versions of some of the utilitarian items of the past. One type eagerly sought by collectors is the knife box *(page 148)*, often elaborately made of polished wood with decorative inlays. A knife box generally has a sloping lid, a serpentine, or curved, front, and slots inside to accommodate flatware. Another finely wrought container is the tea caddy *(page 150)*, a word derived from the Malaysian *kati,* which means a weight of $1\frac{1}{3}$ pounds. Tea imported from Malaysia came in tin, silver or porcelain containers, each holding one *kati.* There are valuable tea caddies of silver and less expensive versions in wood, delftware or lacquered papier-mâché.

The value of a box is, understandably, directly related to the material from which it is made: a silver box will cost more than a tin or copper box. The greater the intrinsic value of a box, the more important its condition. An inlaid and finely veneered box should be in perfect condition, with no veneer or inlay missing. A silver box should not be dented or heavily scratched.

But a brass or copper box of modest design is almost expected to have a few dents, and perhaps some minor

---

The largest of the boxes on the tabletop is the brown 19th Century tea caddy in the center. Also from the 19th Century is the red, lacquered box with brass fittings from the Orient. Most of the others are the small, jewel-like boxes favored by many collectors.

Brass candle boxes like the one above are rarer than wooden ones. This engraved, monogrammed box dates from the 18th Century.

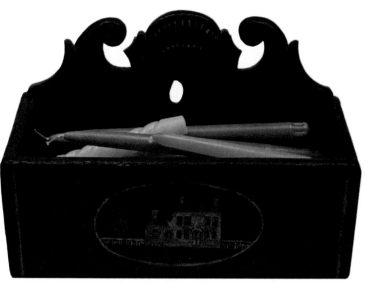

This lidless candle box, designed by a Pennsylvania Dutch craftsman 200 years ago, was made to be hung on the wall.

The sloping lid of the fine 18th Century knife box above opens to reveal padded slots for knives and forks inside. Like most knife boxes, it has a serpentine front and brass handles on the sides.

repairs. It is as if the box's value is proved by the use it has sustained. And wooden salt boxes showing salt stains and a few nicks have lost little value.

Boxes of many kinds can be found not only at antique dealers, but also at flea markets, garage sales and—a source that has been rewarding for me—auctions. Once my daughter and I noticed in a newspaper that the contents of a house across town were to be auctioned off. When we arrived, we saw only two or three people sitting on folding chairs under the trees, and the auctioneer looked dejected. Glancing about, I spotted a charming little box—the figure of a man—on a tabletop full of small things. I was afraid, though, that by singling it out I would draw attention to it and would lose the box to one of the other bidders. So I pounced on an ugly rustic vase and carried both items forward. "Would you put these two things up, please?" I asked. The auctioneer did so, shrugging. "What am I bid?" he asked. No one spoke, so I called out, "A dollar!" "Sold," he said. The little box turned out to be a Kobe dice box made in Japan in the late 19th Century *(page 160)*. Afterward I saw similar ones in shops for as much as $95.

I was less fortunate with another of my searches. I have long expected to find a decoration particularly appropriate to boxes—an illustration of the Greek story of Pandora, who, entrusted with a box she was told not to open, could not resist peeking and so unloosed all of mankind's ills. But I have never seen a box bearing a picture of Pandora. Perhaps you can find one.

For related material, see the articles on Shaker Crafts, Snuff Containers, Tin Containers and Toleware in separate volumes.

The Big Boxes Called Trunks

Trunks and traveling chests are essentially overgrown boxes, and they are prized by many collectors. Some old trunks, like those shown here, can be desirable pieces of furniture, for their brass studs or antique brass bindings and locks are very handsome. And trunks can be used in modern homes to hold everything from winter clothes to snapshot albums.

Leatherbound trunks (*left*) were made by specialists called cofferers, who stretched leather around a wooden frame and "close-nailed" it with special roundheaded brass nails. The leather and studs protected the trunk against the rough handling that luggage must withstand.

Brassbound wooden trunks with hinged lids, like the one below, were popular in America during the stagecoach era, since the trunks were tough enough to take the severe pounding of traveling over crude roads. They were replaced later in the 19th Century, when railroads and steamships became more common, by larger steamer trunks. These, being subject to less wear, were often covered with canvas or oilcloth. The collector of these oversized boxes must beware of one thing: accumulating so many that they take up all the room in the house.

A studded, leather-covered trunk, 10 inches high, has a recycled lining: pages of an old book that were stenciled with polka dots and pasted in. Such use of old paper—even newspapers—was common 150 years ago when paper was scarce.

The pine of a mid-19th Century American trunk still gleams richly, despite its many nicks and scratches. The tiny English olive-wood box in the foreground, made around the turn of the century, was carved to look like an old wooden trunk.

The 19th Century American salt box at right above bears traces of salt stain. The one on the left has a spice drawer. The round sugar box with a lid (center), like the salt boxes, shows the patina and wear of many years of use in country kitchens.

Since tea was an expensive commodity in the 18th and 19th centuries, these three wooden tea caddies all have locks. The octagonal caddy was meant to hold one kind of tea; the double-compartmented caddy (center), two kinds. The long caddy has Oriental decorations.

These 19th Century American pantry boxes are made of bentwood with overlapping seams. They were used to store everything from pills to cheese to herbs. Although pantry boxes are seldom fancy or beautiful, they have the charm of old, useful things.

Hand-forged hardware in a rough tulip pattern secures the lid of a toolbox of the sort Pennsylvanians made for their Conestoga wagons when they set out to migrate west.

This 19th Century Pennsylvania Dutch "bride's box," 18 inches long, has on its lid a folk-art portrayal of a young woman. The box was used to store wedding finery.

The product of an amateur craftsman, this slipper box is wood sheathed with copper. Magazines of the 1890s, like today's, carried directions for such do-it-yourself projects.

Among the more elegant boxes are portable letter-writing desks. The open one shows the lidded compartment for pens and ink. The other has handsome brass corners and inlays.

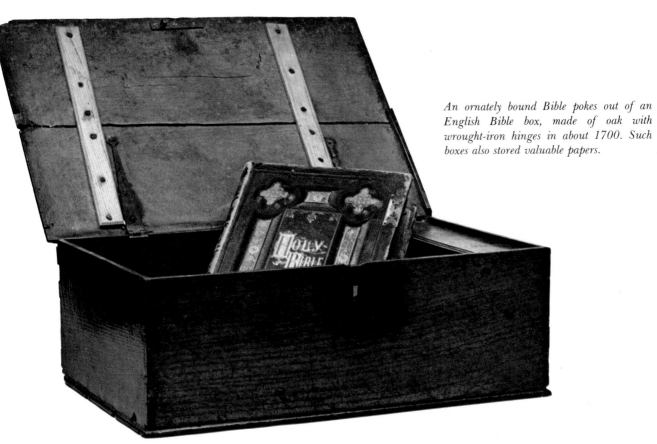

An ornately bound Bible pokes out of an English Bible box, made of oak with wrought-iron hinges in about 1700. Such boxes also stored valuable papers.

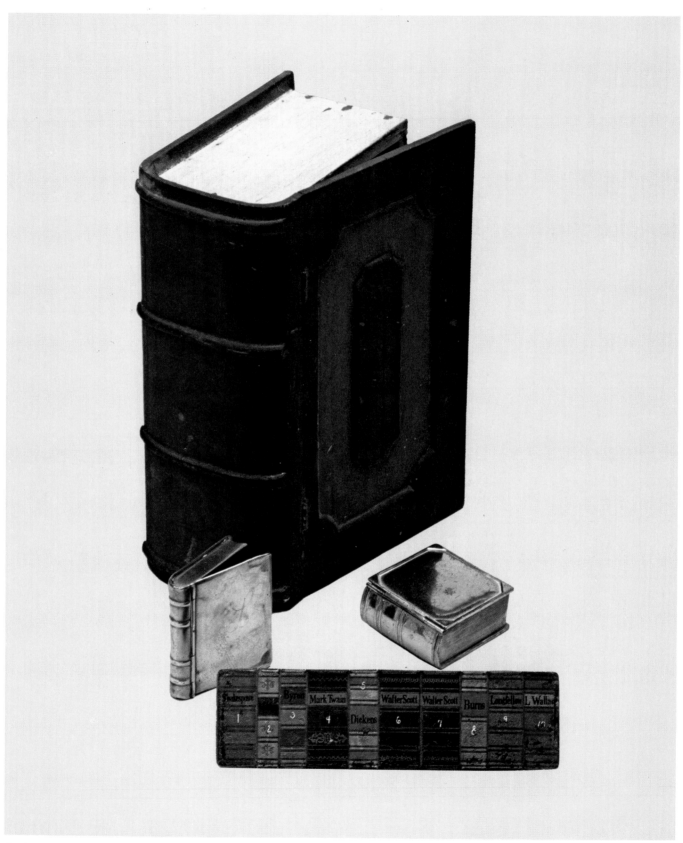

Books are among the myriad shapes boxes have taken. The large wooden and small copper examples were made in England; the small brass one is American. In the foreground is a 19th Century English pencil box decorated with painted book spines.

A wreath-enclosed profile of Princess Mary of England decorates a brass cigarette box that dates from 1914. The box is one of hundreds that the Princess sent as Christmas presents to troops at the front during World War I. The names of the Allied powers appear in cartouches around the lid of this 5⅛-inch-long box.

The brass-and-copper tobacco box above, which was made in the Netherlands for export, is dated 1756. The words that are inscribed on the lid translate, "Spring—Summer—Autumn—Winter— The making of boxes was formerly a great art in our land: but now with us the rustics make them both great and small."

At right above is an early-19th Century snuffbox made of tortoise shell and inlaid with gold, silver and mother-of-pearl. A much later box (left) is painted tin in imitation of this style. The oval tortoise-shell snuffbox has a pierced-heart design on its lid.

An 1890s American glass jewel box, molded by the Pairpont Manu-facturing Company, was decorated by C. F. Monroe & Company.

A porcelain box with a picture of a bridge in Knoxville, Tennessee, came from Germany as one of many souvenirs made for export.

The silver ring box at right above, in the Art Nouveau style popular in about 1900, has a silk lining. The other ring boxes, from the same period, are a jeweler's velvet "presentation box" and a round, black Celluloid box with a miniature portrait on the top.

A jewel box of burled wood has decorations of cast brass set with semi-precious stones and a plaque for the owner's name. It was bought new in France in the 1890s for the collector's mother. The original key still accompanies it—probably because it has stayed with one family.

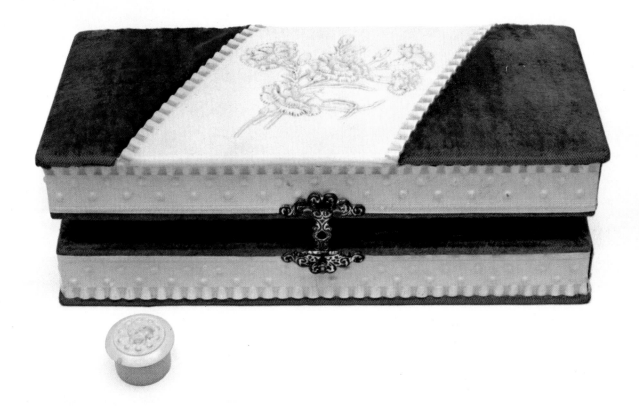

A vanity box, or toilet case, was generally fitted out with a matched set of comb, brush, mirror, nail buffer, scissors, cuticle cutter and salve box (left foreground). This turn-of-the-century example has a puffed satin lining and a molded Celluloid exterior imitating ivory.

Souvenirs brought back from Paris in the 1920s as a gift for the author when she was a child include this handsome Japanese lac-quered perfume box. It has fittings inside to hold two crystal perfume bottles, one of which is shown in the foreground.

This tiny silver vinaigrette has a gold grille that secured a vinegar-scented sponge. It was carried and sniffed to mask street smells.

A heart-shaped brass pillbox made around 1825 is decorated with pewter lovebirds.

Smiles become frowns as the lid of this 1820s patch box is turned 180°, and "before marriage" (in German) becomes "after marriage." Such boxes held beauty spots or face patches.

A silver-decorated lid closes this 2-inch-high ebony powder-puff box made in France.

This veneered hairpin box dating from the 1920s has an inlaid design of swallows and hairpins.

The hat of a carved and painted wood figure forms the lid of this box, made at the turn of the century in the Italian Tyrol.

The eyes move in and out when this dice box from Kobe, Japan, is shaken. The dice are kept in the hat, which doubles as the dice cup.

A thread box from about 1910 has a fortunetelling, clocklike dial on the front. By spinning the hour hand, ladies and gentlemen of the Edwardian period could read their fortunes in love and marriage.

MUSEUMS
Greenfield Village & Henry Ford Museum
Dearborn, Michigan 48121

Old Sturbridge Village
Sturbridge, Massachusetts 01566

Henry Francis Du Pont Winterthur Museum
Winterthur, Delaware 19735

BOOKS
Andere, Mary, *Old Needlework Boxes and Tools.*
Drake Publishers, Inc., 1971.

Bedford, John, *All Kinds of Small Boxes.* Walker
and Company, 1965.

Cole, Brian, *Boxes.* Chilton Book Company,
1976.

Klamkin, Marian, *The Collector's Book of Boxes.*
Dodd, Mead & Company, 1970.

Maust, Don A., ed., *American Woodenware and
Other Primitives.* E. G. Warman Publishing Co., 1974.